DUNBLANE

FROM THE STONE AGE TO MARY QUEEN OF SCOTS

by

BILL INGLIS

To my Wife Valerie

Published by
Jamieson and Munro

ISBN No.
978-0-9569483-0-4

Printed by
The Monument Press, Abbey Road, Riverside, Stirling FK8 1LP

This book has been produced by Jamieson & Munro and production costs were supported by a grant from the Trustees of the John Jamieson Munro Charitable Trust

CONTENTS

ACKNOWLEDGEMENTS

I would like to thank my many friends in Dunblane for their support and encouragement in producing this book. Countless interesting conversations have contributed their part. I am also especially grateful to the trustees of the John Jamieson Munro Charitable Trust for their central contribution to the publication of this book, to the Society of Friends of Dunblane Cathedral who have funded the launch of this book and to the SSE's Braes of Doune Wind Farm Trust for covering the cost of the Scran images which have significantly enhanced its quality. In addition I would like to acknowledge the formal endorsement of the book by the Dunblane Local History Society, the Dunblane Community Council and the Dunblane Civic Society, the last giving financial support.

I owe a great debt to George Dixon, Chief Archivist of the Central Region of Scotland before the re-organisation of the nineties. I have had many discussions with him about the central themes in this book, teasing out the essential issues on which I should concentrate. Len Bovill, Colin Storrar and Ewing Wallace have contributed significantly through their excellent photographs.

I especially appreciate the support of my wife Valerie in prompting me to start, continue and finish and for discussing helpfully each stage as it developed.

Finally I would of course like to emphasise that I am responsible for all the errors of fact, emphasis and argument in this book.

PREFACE

In this book I felt it was essential, despite the shortage of sources, to tackle first the early and mediaeval periods in Dunblane's history and focus on the emergence and working of the Bishopric of Dunblane and on the construction of the Cathedral as crucial to understanding the importance of Dunblane in Scotland's past. I have tried to miss the main traps that local historians find so difficult to avoid.

Every local historian is tempted by the traditional tales and stories that are handed down from generation to generation. The most attractive traditions of this sort in Dunblane are stories about St Blane, of how he set up a monastery inside a fort on Holmhill in Dunblane and how from his base in Bute he conducted a number of missionary journeys like those of St Paul. Unfortunately the founding of the monastery in Dunblane rests on one interpretation of the name Dunblane ie St Blane's fort when that may not have been the original name of the settlement while the stories about the life of St Blane cannot be traced back beyond dubious sources from the late Middle Ages written at least 800 years after St Blane's death. While it is of course sad to have to disillusion people about their favourite local tales it is important for the historian to strip them away and to establish the facts that can be verified and on which cautious speculation can then be built.

Equally dangerous is the temptation for the local historian to ignore or minimise the context of the history that is being described. By "context" I mean the relationship between the local history of a place and of the country where it is located - in this case between the history of Dunblane and that of Scotland. Such a relationship is especially important here because for many years Dunblane was the centre of a Bishopric which though by no means the most important in Scotland still played a significant part in the government of the country.

There is of course another "context" which is often ignored; that of the Bishopric of Dunblane within a larger church. Initially the Bishopric of Dunblane was probably part of the Celtic Church. This Church was based in Ireland but ultimately spread its influence throughout the British Isles and into France and Germany. Then as the power of the Catholic Church grew so the See of Dunblane became part of a Church with its headquarters generally in Rome and which dominated much of Western and Southern Europe. Ultimately at the end of the period covered by this book even this context began to shift with the spread of the Reformation. Even the most ardent Scottish reformers gratefully acknowledged the importance of forces outside Scotland in their success; the inspirational influence of Calvin in Geneva; Henry VIII's break with Rome and his daughter

Elizabeth's support for Protestantism; the power struggle between France and Spain in the middle of the 16th century; and Luther's famous protest against Papal Indulgences in 1517.

There is a further contextual awareness which is essential and relates to the Cathedral. There is little doubt that Dunblane's chief claim to fame is its Cathedral which is one of the three best mediaeval buildings surviving in Scotland. This has to be understood and accepted as part of the Gothic movement which swept from the Île de France to the outermost extent of the British Isles encompassing Dunblane in the process. European and occasionally English architectural historians have tended to downplay this connection largely ignoring the Gothic movement in Scotland. At the same time Scottish writers have tended to see the Gothic movement as indigenous to Scotland and minimise the influences from Europe and south of the border. In this book a strenuous effort will be made to counter both these tendencies.

There is a final pitfall which is a particular danger in a book of this nature and that is to centre it mainly on events in the lives of the leading families in the place being described. In the case of Dunblane during the Middle Ages that would mean focussing almost solely on the actions of the Bishops and ignoring those of the rest of the people. Local historians of mediaeval Scotland are especially exposed to this danger because very few contemporary documents illuminating the social and economic history of the period have survived. This dearth of sources arises partly because of the Wars of Independence which caused such devastation in Scotland and partly by further destruction at the Reformation which for some reason was particularly severe in this country.

Every effort has been made to make the reader aware of the presence of social groups outside the elite in Dunblane. My account of their lives, however, is anything but adequate and so I have taken a drastic and some may consider an unhistorical approach to rectify this imbalance. I have argued towards the end of the book with good reason that there was very little significant change in the agriculture and industry of Scotland between 1350 and 1650. It follows that it is reasonable to draw on the rich collection of late 16th and early 17th century inventories of their goods and household possessions left by tenants and artisans living in Dunblane at that time to describe the probable social and economic structure of Dunblane in the period 1350 to 1560. These inventories were drawn up at death and were used with or without a will by the Commissary Court of Dunblane to validate the value of an individual's possessions and thus ensure that the heirs all received fair treatment. I am aware of the violence I seem to be doing in this instance to normal historical practice but consider it essential so that a balanced picture of the society of Dunblane in the late mediaeval period can be provided.

INTRODUCTION

The foundation and development of Dunblane resulted from its superb strategic position. As can be seen from the map it stands beside what is known as the "Stirling Gap" astride by far the best route from the south to the north of Scotland. To the west the way is blocked by mountains and to the east by a widening River Forth. It is on the road followed by all the armies invading Scotland from the Romans, to William the Conqueror, to Edward 1st and culminating in Cumberland's advance into the Highlands early in 1746 prior to the Battle of Culloden. It is on the main route taken by modern engineers, the railway in the 19th century and the M9/A9 in the 20th century.

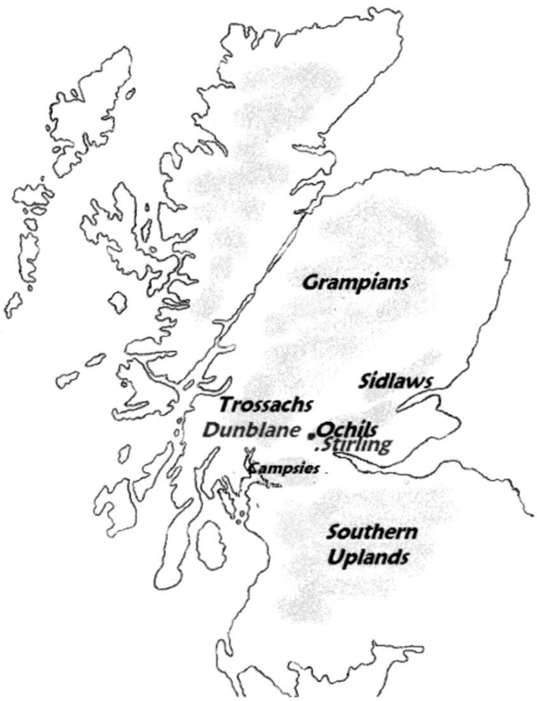

Map showing the importance of Dunblane's geographical position.

Dunblane is of course not just on the main route north it is the first stopping point as you enter and the last as you leave the north of Scotland. In the past this crucial position was far more significant than today. Through Dunblane people gained access not only to the Highlands but also to the rich agricultural lands of Angus, Fife and the shores of the Moray Firth. Historians now accept that the origin of the Kingdom of Scotland was in Pictland, north east of the Forth. As such it was the heartland of the Kingdom to which the Scots retreated in times of national peril and which no invader has been able to subdue. Dunblane was a frontier town on the edge of this inner kingdom.

CHAPTER 1

SCOTLAND AND DUNBLANE IN THE STONE AGE 12,000 - 2,500 BC

The Old and Middle Stone Ages 12,000 - 4,000 BC

The earliest evidence of human activity in Scotland reported recently (2009) is at Howburn near Biggar. Discovered by the Biggar Museum Archaeology Group it consists of flints including scrapers, blades and piercers which have been dated to 12,000 BC. Even though this find has pushed back evidence of man's presence in Scotland 3,000 years it pales beside the traces of early man in Norfolk estimated by Dr Alice Roberts in a recent TV programme to a million years old.

The limited evidence of human settlement in Scotland up to 4,000 BC has also frustrated archaeologists. Very few sites have been identified for this period and the few that have been established were on the fringes of the country – on the coast, up rivers, on the edges of lochs and on islands. Despite this limited evidence archaeologists consider that it is almost certain that by 6,000 BC the whole country and especially the lowlands of Scotland were covered with sites that were occupied and reoccupied over centuries.

Archaeologists offer a range of explanations for their failure to identify more sites. They point out that until 4,000 BC all the inhabitants of Scotland were hunter-gatherers, that is they lived mainly by hunting with some gathering of wild fruits and vegetables in season. The numbers in each group were probably small, no more than a few families at the most who were frequently on the move. Thus at each site the only signs of occupation left behind were piles of stone flakes, burnt stones from the

Reconstruction of the exterior of a shelter used by hunter-gatherers in the Middle Stone Age. (Archaeolink Trust. Licensor www.scran.ac.uk)

hearth and postholes from the stakes, which supported their huts that were covered with animal skins.

These insubstantial traces have been difficult to find since they were quickly covered by the debris of subsequent years and any surviving organic material, which would have helped the archaeologists to date a settlement has been consumed by Scotland's acid soil. When it comes to their failure to find significant numbers of inland sites archaeologists argue that they have been destroyed by subsequent settlement and by farming activity, especially ploughing. Also in jest but with a touch of truth one archaeologist did remark that it was odd that most of the Middle Stone Age sites discovered in Scotland were where archaeologists took their holidays.

In our part of Scotland the discovery of sites follows the national pattern. For example Lorna Main in *First Generations* highlights the extensive activity by people in this period along the River Forth. Thus a series of shell middens dated between 5,000 and 4,000 BC have been discovered on the southern bank of the river below Stirling and on the northern bank at Braehead near Alloa. It is likely that they indicate the sites occupied by groups of hunter-gatherers in the winter season. Similar evidence came to light in the Victorian period when the skeletons of four whales were discovered near Stirling with antler tools beside them. Away from the river evidence of hunter-gatherers is more limited being confined to collections of flints at Bannockburn and a pit at Chapelfield near Cowie.

An archaeologist at a Middle Stone Age dump near Polmont containing the remains of food, for example shellfish eaten by hunter-gatherers.
(Scotsman Publications Ltd. Licensor www.scran.ac.uk)

Not surprisingly evidence of hunter-gatherer activity in Dunblane is limited. There is no doubt that the hunter-gatherers will have passed through the area covered by Dunblane today. Archaeologists consider that they favoured bluffs beside salmon rivers where they could fish as well as hunt inland. Dunblane has many such sites but none have yet yielded any evidence of occupation during the Middle Stone Age. In the town itself there is however some tantalising evidence reported in the *Transactions of the Stirling Natural History and Antiquarian Society 1892-93.* During drainage work in Kirk Street workers cutting into a peat moss found three fragments of antler bone with evidence of having been worked into tools by man. The whereabouts of these remains are not known. Also in the first half of the 20th century two shaped claystone axes which may come from the Middle Stone Age were discovered in the River Allan and deposited in the Smith Institute, Stirling.

Flint axe from the Middle Stone Age.
(Dumfries and Galloway Museum Service. Licensor www.scran.ac.uk)

The New Stone Age 4,000 - 2,500 BC

The Introduction of Farming 4,000 - 3,500 BC

The most important change in Scotland's history prior to the Industrial Revolution of the 18th and 19th centuries AD – the introduction of farming – took place between 4,000 BC and 3,500 BC. People changed from being nomadic hunter-gatherers who moved with the supply of game and the rhythm of the seasons to having their base in one place throughout the year. Instead of hunting, and all the activities associated with exploiting the carcass of an animal, mankind was tied to the annual production of crops and tending herds of domesticated animals. It is likely that this vital transition was forced on mankind by a sharp increase in the population, which could only be supported by intensive farming. There is also little doubt that for most people the change was for the worse with longer and more monotonous hours of work ensuring that in general people were less healthy apparently being physically smaller and living shorter lives in the new era.

Farming was introduced into Scotland very late. In the Near East, admittedly the first place where farming emerged, it was established as early as 8,500 BC and took a further 4,000 years (4,500 BC) to become predominant throughout Western Europe. In Scotland it was even more delayed taking a further 500 years (4,000 BC) before there is evidence that hunter-gatherers and farmers had started to exist side by side. It took a further 250 years (3,750 BC) for farming to become predominant south of Angus and in Northern Perthshire and another 250 years (3,500 BC) for it to be general across the whole country. However once established the range of crops; wheat, barley and oats and of animals; horses, oxen, cows and sheep was little different from farms as late as the middle of the 20th century except of course for the yield of the crops and the size of the animals.

The remains of two houses dating from 3600 BC at Knap of Howar, Orkney. Their occupants kept cattle, sheep and pigs and grew oats and barley.
(Historic Scotland. Licensor www.scran.ac.uk)

The introduction of farming settlements from c 4,000 BC in Scotland has led to a far richer survival of archaeological evidence than resulted from the sites occupied by hunter-gatherers. With farming houses became more substantial and permanent with their remains being more evident than previously. Domestic and farm tools became more sophisticated and occasionally have been discovered on site. At the same time with a more settled existence evidence of community life in the form of human burials and stone circles have survived.

Our knowledge of New Stone Age settlements on the mainland of Scotland is very limited. Based on a very small number of survivals in the British Isles it has been assumed that the houses were small and regular as opposed to the sophisticated circular stone houses with their stone bed recesses, stone dressers and stone tables found so spectacularly at Scara Brae; the evidence especially for the Scottish mainland is insufficient, however to reach a firm conclusion.

The picture has been further complicated by the discovery of three examples of a completely different kind of house in Scotland from this period – large elaborate timber hall houses that would have provided accommodation for a sizeable extended family or a number of nuclear families. Intriguingly this type of house was very common in the Netherlands, northwest France and Ireland. Until recently there were only two examples known in Scotland at Balbridie in Aberdeenshire dated to 3,900 to 3,750 BC and at Whitmuirhaugh on the Scottish Borders.

From the point of view of those concerned with the history of Dunblane and its locality it is interesting that the third example of this kind of house found in Scotland was discovered by aerial photography in 1977 at Claish Farm about a mile south of Callander, although it was not excavated until 2001. The results of the excavation were reported in an article by Gordon J Barclay, Kenneth Brophy and Gavin MacGregor published in *History Scotland Vol. 2 No. 1 Jan/Feb 2002.* The building was 25 metres long and 9 metres broad, a substantial construction by any standards. Inside was evidence of partitions dividing the house or dwelling into five chambers, one of which had two fire pits with the remains of cereals, especially wheat. The broken pieces of what was probably one large round bottomed Neolithic bowl were found on the site.

The greater sophistication of the people of the New Stone Age has led to the survival of a range of artefacts, examples of which have been discovered in and nearby Dunblane. At this time pottery appeared for the first time, initially simple round bottomed bowls, which became more elaborate with time and then grooved ware, the groove being brought about by running a finger round the edge of the vessel. The only grooved ware found in the Stirling area has been at Barbush in Dunblane. At the same time more sophisticated tools were developed for example ploughs, axes and even querns, usually consisting of two stones that were used to grind corn, have been found. In our area beautiful polished axes have been discovered at Braes Farm in the Braes of Doune.

Photograph revealing the ground plan of the hall house at Balbridie in Aberdeenshire after excavation.
(National Museums Scotland. Licensor www.scran.ac.uk)

Burial chambers, stone circles and standing stones 3,000 - 2,500 BC
Starting around 4,000 BC and spreading right across Scotland there is a proliferation of large mounds and stone chambers for the burial of the dead. Excavations have shown that a number of individuals either from one family or a local community were buried in these mounds or chambers together. It is also likely that the sites were reused many times over the centuries.

In some parts of Scotland these burial monuments appear to have reached high aesthetic standards and to be of religious significance. In this connection Maes Howe on the Isle of Orkney is perhaps Scotland's if not Britain's finest chambered tomb. As can be seen below the chamber was exquisitely constructed with large sandstone blocks. It also appears to be associated with the worship of the sun since it is designed around a long passage, which points to the setting of the sun during the days around mid-winter. To facilitate this a blocking stone was placed in the middle of the passage allowing the setting sun to shine through a horizontal slit, creating a bar of light on the back wall of the chamber.

Maes Howe on the Isle of Orkney.

Locally we have a profusion of these burial monuments although none reach the standard attained by Maes Howe. They are generally constructed with large stone slabs along the sides and dividing the chamber into compartments. Close by at Auchenlaich near Callander are the remains of the longest chambered cairn in Scotland, presumably the chambers contained the dead. At Cromlix in Dunblane there is a long cairn from this period but without there being any evidence of a chamber.

Auchenlaich Chambered Cairn.
The line of the cairn is marked by three bushes,
two large and one small running diagonally
across the middle of the image.
(Royal Commission for Ancient and Historical Monuments Scotland (RCAHMS).
Licensor www.scran.ac.uk)

The Neolithic period also saw the emergence of stone circles, lines of stones and single standing stones. Their likely purpose was for communal ceremonies probably of a religious nature. Their initial construction was towards the end of the Neolithic period and may have continued into the Bronze Age, that is after 2,500 BC. Construction of these remarkable monuments swept across Britain but they are only now present, or have only survived, in parts of Scotland, mainly on the islands of the north, though we are fortunate in Dunblane to have a number of such monuments in the parish or very nearby. Perhaps the best-known stone circle in Scotland is Knap of Howar on the Isle of Orkney.

The purpose of these monuments is still not clear. It has been established that they are linked to the movements of the sun and the moon but there is no way of confirming that the people who erected the stone circles worshipped the sun and moon though it is a reasonable supposition. It is also likely that the circles were associated with the main agricultural phases of the year and that fertility rituals were conducted there.

Ring of Brodgar, Scotland's largest stone circle.
(Diego Meozzi. Licensor www.scran.ac.uk)

Some people, like Professor Thom writing some forty years ago, have gone much further and have postulated that the people who built the stone circles had a sophisticated knowledge of astronomy. They have observed that there are many alignments with the stars possible from different stones in a circle. They have even suggested that major sites may have been used as places where would-be Stone Age astronomers were instructed by well-informed teachers. Sceptics have pointed out that the alignments proposed by Professor Thom and his followers are dependant on which stones are selected at a particular site and that there is no way of determining whether they have been positioned deliberately.

A more profitable approach has been to examine the social significance of these monuments. It is interesting that they appear to be the first communal structures erected by man in Scotland. Some of the smaller ones will have been for local use, the inhabitants of a few farmsteads only, but the bigger ones often placed on hills so that they can be seen from a long way off will have drawn people from a distance. If as seems virtually certain they were erected for a religious purpose their existence implies that society at the time was theocratic, in other words dominated by priests not by a warrior elite. The second half of this assertion is confirmed by the complete absence of forts and defended settlements at this time. To us it seems very strange that human society in Scotland

Part of a Stone Circle at Temple near Kilmartin, unusually including burials.

could exist without people fighting for the available resources of the country and that societies could co-exist without being in continual tension. Yet this was the case for hundreds of years in the Stone Age and even in some countries like Scotland in the Bronze Age. The explanation usually offered is that there was no population pressure on the available resources so there was no need for kings, chiefs and warriors.

In Dunblane, or very close by, we have the remains of four stone monuments from this period *viz.*

- a line of stones at Lairhill, just beside Sheriffmuir,
- a single standing stone at Glenhead Farm and a line of standing stones near by - Glenhead Farm is between Dunblane and Doune.
- a standing stone at Whiteston Farm, north of Dunblane off the Perth Road.

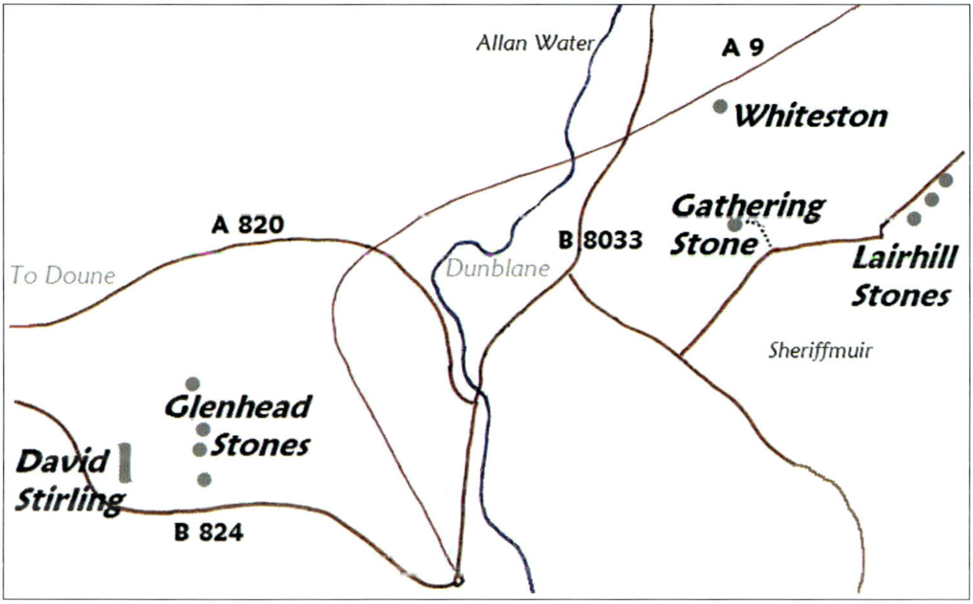

Map showing the location of standing stones in and around Dunblane.

The line of stones, which would have been most dramatic when first erected is on Lairhill, NE of the Sheriffmuir Inn. If you are interested in "re-discovering" them you should first walk to the only stone that is standing approaching it from the west. It is clearly visible from the Dunblane and Bridge of Allan roads as you near the Inn. Once you reach the standing stone turn ENE and about 75 yards away you will see a large stone flat on its side. Then turn round and retrace your steps to the standing stone. Continue on the line, which runs ENE-WSW made by the two stones and you will find the remains of four other stones. The first two are difficult to find, and are not very convincing, but the last two are large and clearly part of the monument. There is a possible seventh stone over a hundred yards further on. Barty notes that the stones are called the Wallace Stones because of a tradition that they were erected to record an engagement between Wallace and the English at the site – needless to say Wallace won. Barty, like all reliable authorities, discounts this tale dating the monument from prehistoric time.

The only stone left standing at Lairhill.

The single standing stone at Glenhead Farm is about fifty yards east of the farm at the edge of a small wood. The stone faces NNE-SSW and it is likely that it has always been a lone standing stone because there is no evidence of other stones nearby. It is perhaps the most dramatic of all the stones in and near Dunblane because you come upon it unusually in a wood. Like other standing stones in Scotland and elsewhere it has a number of hollows on its surface. Archaeologists describe them as cup markings because of their shape and regard them as contemporary with the early use of the stones.

The single standing stone at Glenhead Farm.

(photograph by Colin Storrar)

From the single standing stone you can walk to the line of standing stones that are near to Glenhead Farm. Return to the farm and follow the path to the south of the farm skirting a wood. After about a quarter of a mile you will enter an open field with the statue of Sir David Stirling to your right. Halfway across the field you will see the line of standing stones to your left. There are three of them like the single standing stone at the farm facing NNE-SSW. The most southerly stone is well over six feet high. The second stone has a flat top with cup markings on its surface. The third stone is also about six feet high but is broken. Finally you will find a fourth stone lying on the ground. All four stones are very close together and this monument appears altogether more intimate and less grand than the one on Lairhill will have been in its heyday.

A particularly good view of two of the three standing stones that are still upright near Glenhead Farm with Dunblane in the middle distance.
(photograph by Colin Storrar)

On the opposite side of the parish just south of Upper Whitestone Farm off the Perth Road is the biggest standing stone in or near Dunblane. It is at least 8 feet tall and four feet wide and stands in proud isolation with the hills of Sheriffmuir behind it.

Finally there is the Gathering Stone on Sheriffmuir. There is no reliable evidence on the origin or purpose of this stone except that it certainly predates the battle of Sheriffmuir.

It is very difficult to assess the importance of these stone monuments. No special significance should be attached to the number at or near Dunblane. It is likely that they were common elsewhere in the Stirling area and up the River Allan, surviving by accident in Dunblane. It is also difficult to interpret these individual monuments since stones may have been removed from some of the sites. As a result there may have been many other such monuments in Dunblane in the late Stone Age. One hypothesis can be ventured however.

It is not unreasonable to suggest that the single standing stones were of less communal significance than the lines and circles of stones, possibly catering for people living in one or two settlements while the bigger monuments were for groups of settlements. In this connection the line of stones at Lairhill will have stood out on the skyline as people approached from all sides. Even today the single stone still standing is a dramatic sight as you cross the small bridge over the Ault Wharrie Burn to the south west of Lairhill.

The standing stone at Upper Whitestone Farm with Sheriffmuir behind it.
(photograph by Colin Storrar)

CHAPTER 2

SCOTLAND AND DUNBLANE IN THE BRONZE AGE 2500 - 750 BC

Working in Bronze - trade and its social consequences

The central feature of the Bronze Age was the production of bronze, a mixture of copper and tin. The two raw materials were melted at a very high temperature, poured into a mould of stone and then finished by hand polishing or sharpening as appropriate. As a result man was able to make personal ornaments, tools and weapons of a very high standard of craftsmanship. For example the Sumerian, Egyptian and Cretan civilizations were creations of the Bronze Age.

Mould for making an axe-head dated 1800-1100 BC found at New Deer, Aberdeenshire. The red colouring on the stone may be caused by the heat of the liquid bronze.

(University of Aberdeen. Licensor www.scran.ac.uk)

Such heights were not reached in Scotland. The population was still very small and thinly spread across the country. Archaeologists reckon that even in 2,000 BC there was probably only one settlement or at the most a small group of settlements per half mile in Scotland and there were of course no towns or villages. However there is clear evidence even in Scotland that the new skills were put to effective use.

There is, for example, a growth in a whole range of ornaments for personal adornment such as pins, buttons, necklaces and brooches. The production of these luxury items rested on a surprisingly sophisticated system of international trade. Thus while copper was available locally in Scotland the nearest supply of tin was in Southern England making production of bronze a very expensive procedure. This trade was supplemented by the import of other luxuries for example of gold jewellery from Ireland and jet from the area of modern Whitby in the North of England. As a consequence these ornaments were much prized and only available to the elite of society.

To judge by the surviving grave goods an elite had emerged in Scotland during the Bronze Age distinguishable by their ownership of these luxury items. Their existence signals a change in society from the communities of the late Stone Age led by priests who officiated at their stone monuments to a Bronze Age elite who were laymen. It is clear from recent excavations at

Barbush which will be described below that some members of that latter elite lived in what is now Dunblane.

Farming, houses and burial practices

Between 2,500 and 1,500 BC agriculture improved in Scotland. The climate especially between 2,000 and 1,500 BC was warmer than today making it possible to extend farming well into the Scottish Uplands. There traces of the circular huts inhabited by people during the Bronze Age are still visible when such remains have long since been destroyed by ploughing in the lowlands.

In the centre of the photograph is a probable Bronze Age hut circle in the Perthshire hills at Pitcarmick, Kirkmichael.

(RCAHMS Licensor www.scran.ac.uk)

The warmth of the weather combined with improved tools through working in bronze enhanced farming. Better ploughs came into use though they were still stone tipped. At Loch Nell in Argyll an ox-yoke has been found dating to this period showing that draught animals were used for the first time. Previously people had dragged the ploughs. Light harrows for weeding have been discovered. Barley appears to have been the predominant crop in much of the country at this time as opposed to oats which has normally been the main crop in Scotland because of the short summer. Surprisingly there may even have been a degree of specialisation with cattle being the dominant agricultural product on the Isle of Harris, an early sign of Highland predominance in the production of livestock.

Changes were also apparent in the types of houses constructed during this period. About 2,000 BC houses everywhere in Scotland, except for Orkney and Shetland, became circular as opposed to rectangular and more elaborate than previously. At the centre of the house which had no inner walls were the fireplace, cooking trough and the oven. The outer walls were constructed of a base of stone surmounted by turf and soil held together by a ring of stout stakes. The walls supported a conical thatch or straw roof. Inside, areas were partitioned by walls made of stone and turf lined with a wooden fence and they were used for a wide range of purposes including keeping animals.

Burial practices also changed during the Bronze Age. The communal burials of the Stone Age were replaced by individual burials which might be cremations in which case the remains were placed in a large pot or else inhumations, that is internment of the intact body of the individual. The remains were normally placed in what archaeologists describe as a cist that is a shallow grave lined with large stone slabs one of which was placed over the grave. Along side the body a food vessel was often laid which might contain gruel or a flavoured drink. Remains of a joint of pork have even been found in one grave. In addition personal possessions were placed beside the body including items like daggers, archery equipment and jewellery. Recently archaeologists concluded that a Bronze Age burial discovered at Forteviot had flowers in the grave. A significant number of cists have been discovered in Dunblane which will be described below.

Climate change and its consequences 1,500 - 500 BC

It is clear that between 1,500 and 500 BC there was considerable climatic decline in Scotland though as with much writing on the history of the climate considerable disagreement occurs on its timing. Some authorities state that much cooler and wetter weather affected the country before 1,000 BC others see it happening much closer to 500 BC. They do however agree that the weather did deteriorate initially to become like our own and then possibly poorer. It is also accepted that during this period, because of the worsening conditions and peat covering much of the Scottish uplands, arable farming became very difficult.

The deteriorating climate reduced the area available for cultivation leading to the intensification of agriculture on the lower ground. It was no longer possible to cultivate the higher ground as previously and people were forced to leave the upland areas. Oaks and other types of natural vegetation which had been absent for centuries reappeared on the hills. Land which was difficult to cultivate was broken in more extensively than previously, using draught animals. Probably arising from increased pressure on the land the first clearly demarcated fields with banks of stone and earth were created to establish boundaries and ownership. Eventually the farming was so intensive that by the end of the Bronze Age there is some evidence of soil erosion in Scotland.

The social impact of these changes was considerable. Competition for land led for the first time to evidence of defended settlements across Scotland for example at Portknockie on the Moray Firth, Myrehead at Falkirk, and in the east of Scotland at Eildon Hill and Dryburn Bridge all erected in the 8th century BC. Such settlements quickly became general especially in the area around Dunblane and will be considered when the Iron Age is described below.

Bronze Age cist burials in Dunblane

In Dunblane eleven cist burials from the Bronze Age have been found. In chronological order they were discovered as follows:

- in 1879 four while building the Glenallan Cottages in Dunblane
- in 1901 one 500 yards west of Cromlix House (now hotel)
- in 1903 one during the building of the Cathedral Hall
- in 1928 one a few feet from the north west corner of the Cathedral
- in 1975 one a few metres west of the Cathedral Chapter House
- in 2000 three at Barbush Quarry during house building

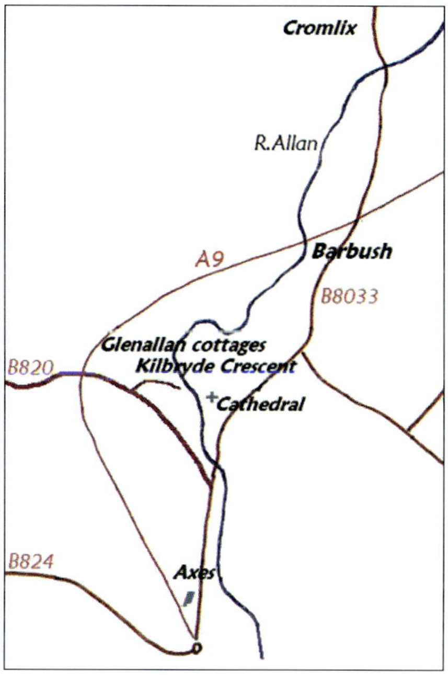

Map of Dunblane showing the sites where cists have been found and also Bronze Age axe heads. (see below)

A number of these cists yielded nothing or virtually nothing. Two of the four discovered when the Glenallan Cottages were being built were destroyed by the workers before their significance was realised. The one found close to Cromlix House was empty. Nothing was found in the cists discovered at the Cathedral Hall and near the Cathedral except for two human teeth in the former. The cist discovered to the north of the Cathedral Chapter House in 1975 contained bones but they were almost certainly from much later mediaeval and early modern burials since the stone covering the cist was missing.

The finds in the two cists that were not destroyed at the Glenallan Cottages were of some significance. One contained a food vessel on which there was some decoration and the other contained a bronze dagger. The bronze dagger was 11.8 by 4.1 cm with three rivet holes at its head, two with the rivets still in place. Unfortunately this find appears to have been lost so it is not possible to verify its quality or likely date but it was clearly from the Bronze Age.

By far the most important finds have been from Barbush. There in 1999 three cists were unearthed containing between them a skeleton, a pot and a necklace. The skeleton was extremely fragile disintegrating on touch and could not be saved. The pot which was in pieces when it was found has been reconstructed. It was a crudely decorated food vessel from c 2000 BC of a sort that is often found in Bronze Age graves and may have contained some food or drink for the deceased's after-life.

The necklace of a similar date was by far the most spectacular find. It was made of cannel-coal, a bituminous fuel, that is it burns with a bright light, a most unusual material for a necklace. When it was found the necklace was loose and comprised 124 discs of coal which formed the beads of the ornament. Each disc had a hole in its centre which had been neatly drilled and they were all subtly graded with the largest in the centre and the smallest at either end. While the cannel coal was local the fastener was of Whitby jet. Since Whitby is 275 km. from Dunblane the presence of the jet is evidence of the long distance trade of the Bronze Age. The necklace which is complete had its outer surface polished and to judge by the wear on the fastener had been in use for some time. Since the necklace is small and of very fine workmanship it is likely that it belonged to a child of a high status family. Other necklaces and ornaments have been found for this period but the Barbush necklace is probably the finest. It is displayed along with the pot at Dunblane Museum.

The Bronze Age necklace found at Barbush

(By kind permission of Dunblane Museum. photograph by Ewing Wallace)

Bronze Age axe heads found in Dunblane

Axe heads, the other common category of Bronze Age finds, have also been unearthed in Dunblane. In September 1964 Mr. D. Sinclair from Gargunnock discovered a Bronze Age axe head when laying the foundation of a wall in Kilbryde Crescent. The find was 125 yards away from the four cists discovered at Glenallan Cottages in 1879. The axe head was flanged, that is it had a broad projecting rim, it was blue green in colour and slightly pitted with a cutting edge 66 mm in length. It was deposited in the Smith Museum. In 2004 Mr Colin Irvine and Mr Jim Smith while metal detecting in a field to the south of Dunblane quite close to the Keir Roundabout discovered four early Bronze Age axe heads. Two were close together and may be part of a hoard and the other two were single deposits and one was decorated. More recently a fifth Bronze Age axe head has been discovered at the same site by Mr. A. Cameron also while metal detecting. All five have been deposited in the Dunblane Museum.

Bronze Age axe head found in a field to the south of Dunblane.

(By kind permission of Dunblane Museum. photograph by Len Bovill)

CHAPTER 3

IRON AGE SCOTLAND AND DUNBLANE UNTIL THE ROMAN INVASION 750 BC - 79 AD

Introduction to the Iron Age

More is known about the Iron Age in Scotland than earlier periods. This greater understanding is not just because it is more recent but also because with the Roman occupation of England and attempted conquest of Scotland we have been provided with written, albeit biased, descriptions of life in Scotland to supplement the archaeological evidence.

The discovery of iron about 500 BC was of great significance. A far stronger and more durable metal than bronze its introduction brought about important changes in agriculture, in warfare and in domestic manufacture. The availability of ore virtually everywhere gave communities more independence since they were no longer reliant on the transport of a component like tin over long distances. At the same time production based entirely on local materials made iron cheaper to produce than bronze and thus ensured that items like agricultural tools were accessible to a wider community.

Iron Age society in Scotland

When the Romans arrived in 79 AD they encountered a tribal society in Scotland. Ptolemy acting on reports from the army recorded the names of 16 tribes in Scotland. It is now accepted that the Damnonii with their capital probably at Dumbarton Rock dominated Central Scotland and accordingly the area of modern Dunblane.

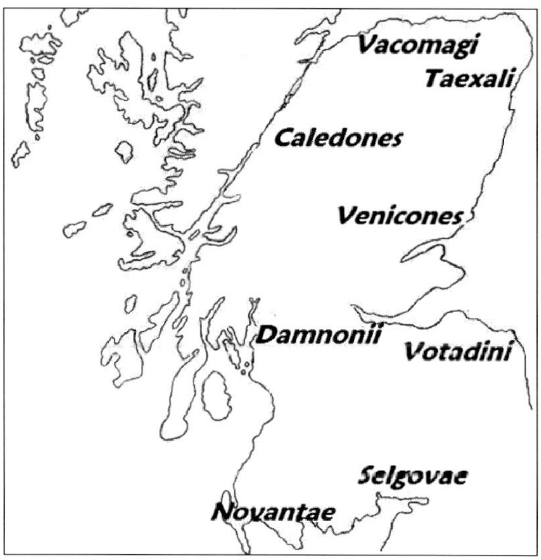

Some of the tribes inhabiting Scotland in 79 AD as named by Ptolemy the geographer.

As a tribal society Scotland was markedly behind Southern Britain where on their arrival the Romans found peoples with kings, towns and even coinage issued by the ruler. An article recently published in the Independent has even described the discovery of a road built by the Britons before the arrival of the Romans which was almost as sophisticated as a Roman road. In Scotland the tribes were without kings or significant leaders. Tacitus' account of Agricola's invasion north of the Solway makes this plain. It is only at the very end of Agricola's campaign that the gathering of tribes before the battle of Mons Graupius were able to elect a leader, Calgacus, literally "the swordsman" who clearly was selected for his military prowess. No other leader is named on the native side during the whole campaign which lasted five years. It is likely then that the leaders of the tribes were groups of senior men, probably land owners, who met to make decisions when they were needed.

Despite the differences between the tribal leadership in North and South Britain they seemed to have shared many characteristics which also extended to tribes on the continent of Europe. Most important they were a warrior aristocracy. According to Roman accounts and from abundant archaeological evidence this elite armed themselves with large slashing swords, rode horses and chariots, loved feasting and drinking, and decorated themselves with magnificent ornaments like armlets and spiral bracelets. The spectacular nature of these ornaments in our part of Scotland has recently (2009) been demonstrated by the discovery of four superb gold neck rings, or torcs, in a field near Stirling. Writing in *History Scotland (Vol.10 No. 2 March/April 2010)* Fraser Hunter describes the find as the most important Iron Age gold hoard found in Scotland. It consists of two ribbon torcs of Scottish or Irish style and two annular, that is ring, torcs. One of them is of a style common in South West France near Toulouse and the other is of a very complex Mediterranean style. The two latter torcs were either imported or produced by local craftsmen who had been as far as France or the Mediterranean to learn their craft.

Replica of a carnyx or war trumpet found at Deskford in Aberdeenshire.

(National Museums of Scotland. Licensor www.scran.ac.uk)

In Scotland it is likely that the warrior aristocracy had undergone some change between 700 BC and the arrival of the Romans. The development of fortifications in the late Bronze Age as pressure on the land increased has already been described. During the period up to the third century BC fortification appears to have intensified. It has been suggested that this reflects a period of insecurity with the country dominated by local warrior landowners. However from about 250 BC most of these fortifications appear to have been abandoned implying that power was centralised at about this time into fewer hands removing the need for local forts.

We know less about the other groups in society. Almost as important as the warrior class were the Druids or priests of the Iron Age tribe. We know very little for certain about this stratum in Iron Age society and most of the information we do have is from their enemies, the Romans. It is likely, however, that they had a long training, and were the teachers, judges and doctors of their tribes as well as the advisers of the tribal kings or leaders. They do not appear to have built temples, their ceremonies taking place in the open at significant sites such as springs which were considered sacred or mountain tops. They seem to have been feared. Certainly the Romans saw them as their most determined and irreconcilable opponents. Of considerable importance also were the craftsmen who provided the elite with their visible signs of status and authority.

The remainder of Iron Age Society is more shadowy. It is now accepted that at least among the relatively undeveloped tribes inhabiting Scotland an influential and very numerous group will have been the tenants of the warrior aristocracy. They will have been mainly subsistence farmers though they will have produced enough to pay their rent to the landowners in kind that is crops and animals. It is likely that they were also liable for military service with their lord and for the tribe as a whole. They will have comprised the free men of the society and may have had a say at least in local decision making. The final group of society and almost certainly the most numerous will have been the landless labourers who were either the servants or slaves of the landowners and tenants.

Forts and fortifications

The warrior aristocracy at least in the early centuries of the Iron Age constructed forts and defended dwellings. The forts were often spectacularly

White Caterthun an Iron Age Fort in Angus with an impressive stone enclosure and possibly two defensive walls.
(RCAHMS. Licensor www.scran.ac.uk)

sited. Generally they had three or more ditches and a stone rampart buttressed by horizontal timber. The two most impressive forts possibly in the whole of Scotland were at Eildon Hill in modern Roxburghshire, the capital of the Selgovae tribe, and Traprain Law in East Lothian capital of the Votadini. The former covered 40 acres and had three miles of fortifications, the latter, in a very striking position, was occupied from 1,000 BC its fortifications and the houses within its walls being rebuilt on numerous occasions. Other forts had intimidating features. At Finavon in Angus the walls probably stood 18 feet high, the forts at Brown and White Caterthun dominated access to Strathmore while at Burghhead in Moray a large promontory fort was constructed, a site which was to be re-used as a naval base by the Picts. In contrast there were small defended settlements as at Dryburn Bridge in East Lothian with only one or two round houses within, almost certainly fortified farm houses.

As if to emphasise the strategic importance of Dunblane and the area around it the sites of five Iron Age forts have been identified in or close to the town. Three overlook the Forth valley, one is between Bridge of Allan and Dunblane and one is within the parish itself. The last two have yet to be confirmed as Iron Age forts by excavation and it is unlikely that all five were occupied at the same time.

The most spectacular is the fort on Dumyat literally "the hill of the Miathi". It stands approximately 400 metres above sea level on a rocky promontory at the top of a hill above Blairlogie dominating the Forth valley. It is in a superb defensive position with steep rock falls to the south and evidence of two walls to the west. The Miathi were in conflict with the Romans in the early third century AD and were still the dominant tribe in the area in the 7th century. A fort on Abbey Craig also occupied a dominant position and traces of its defences can still be seen to the rear of the Wallace Monument. Part of it has been excavated recently and the remains show signs of vitrification. It is generally accepted that vitrification, a form of burning, was carried out by people who captured a fort to demonstrate to the local population that the original chiefs or lords of the locality were no longer in power. There was also a fort on Mote Hill beside Stirling Castle which like the fort on Dumyat had stone walls.

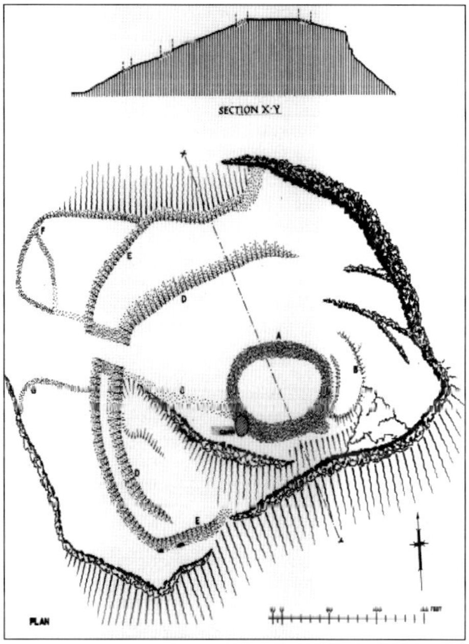

Diagram and section of the Iron Age fort on Dumyat, note the two walls either side of the entrance and the cliffs to the south.
(RCAHMS. Licensor www.scran.ac.uk)

The other two forts are on less spectacular sites. Using the Ordinance Survey Map the first fort can be found between Dunblane and Bridge of Allan about a quarter of a mile directly south of Park of Keir NS 782 984. It lies at the top of a small wooded knoll between two substantial woods. Unfortunately when you climb to the top of the small hill the remains of the fort are very indistinct. Round the edge of the hill you can see what might be the remains of a rampart but it is difficult to be certain. Also the site is much smaller than the three overlooking the Forth. The second fort which is in the parish of Dunblane is also something of a puzzle. Again it is marked on the Ordinance Survey Map about a quarter of a mile north east of Park of Keir NS 781 999 on the very edge of the Kippenross estate. It occupies a surprisingly spectacular site being D shaped with the upright of the D being a hundred foot sheer drop to the river below. The two reports by the Royal Commission of Ancient and Historical Monuments Scotland (RCAHMS) in 1959 and 1969 state that the only remains are of two ramparts to the north of the site. The report of 1959 states that the inner rampart was probably faced with stone, an observation which could not be confirmed in 1969. The interior of the fort is quite large 90 by 55 metres and on balance the RCAHMS consider there was an Iron Age fort at the site. On a recent visit to the site I could not identify ramparts to the north but there were signs of ditches to the west so it is difficult to reach firm conclusions.

Photograph of the wooded knoll to the south of the Park of Keir on which there was probably an Iron Age fort.

Recently archaeologists have been considering the significance of Iron Age forts some of which are spectacular. Does it mean that there was serious conflict or threat of conflict in the early centuries of the Iron Age? That appears to be the case though recently an additional explanation has been offered. It has been pointed out that from the Iron Age until the late Middle Ages castles were built as statements of power as well as defensive positions. They were designed to impress the inhabitants of the area and its visitors with the might and magnificence of the King or local grandee. For example driving on the A9 from the Keir roundabout you are aware of the dominance of Stirling castle for at least five miles. Archaeologists have argued that chiefs and noblemen in the Iron Age would have aimed to achieve the same effect. They point out that a number of Iron Age forts while occupying magnificent positions are not sited well defensively. For example the Iron Age fort at Chesters near Hadrian's Wall is overlooked by higher ground. Surprisingly this is also true of the Iron Age fort on the top of Dumyat. Then the fort at Brown Caterthun near to White Caterthun had nine entrances, hardly ideal for defence. Finally very few hill forts north of the Tay are in commanding defensive positions but they would have looked impressive.

The Iron Age Fort is on the hill to the left of the summit of Dumyat showing how the fort was overlooked by higher ground.
(British Geological Survey. Licensor www.scran.ac.uk)

Iron Age agriculture and houses

Perhaps the greatest impact of the new metal iron was on agriculture. With new tools heavy soils which are a major feature of the land in Scotland could now be cultivated. This led to an intensification of grain farming at least in the East of Scotland. Four poster granary buildings have been identified according to Ian Armit at Broxmouth and Dryburn in East Lothian and at Douglasmuir and Ironshill in Angus. It is likely that the mysterious souterrains, extensive underground chambers built at this time and numerous in the rich corn lands of Angus and east Perthshire were used for this purpose. Their size between 15 and 25 metres in length and up to 2 metres in depth makes it likely that they were for storing the crops of a whole community as opposed to those of one farm. Herds of cattle and flocks of sheep also were kept with evidence of grazing at surprisingly high elevations. Even deer herds appear to have been managed.

Aerial view of the souterrain at Ardestie near Monifieth. Inside the enclosure to the left is the souterrain and to the right the remains of Iron Age huts 1st-2nd century AD.
(RCAHMS. Licensor www.scran.ac.uk)

This increased agricultural activity had a number of consequences. It almost certainly led to the clearing of forest in Lowland Scotland between 300 and 200 BC so that the extent of woodland was similar to that of today. There is also evidence from pollen analysis of cultivation returning to the higher ground in Scotland quite suddenly about 250 BC for example in the Cheviots. Similar trends are evident in Northern England and in the Solway. Archaeologists have argued that the reoccupation of the uplands shows that all the available land which could be cultivated lower down was in use. Perhaps more tendentiously they have suggested that this exploitation of the higher ground reveals that a centralised power had emerged in society capable of organising such a development, an argument which has already been outlined.

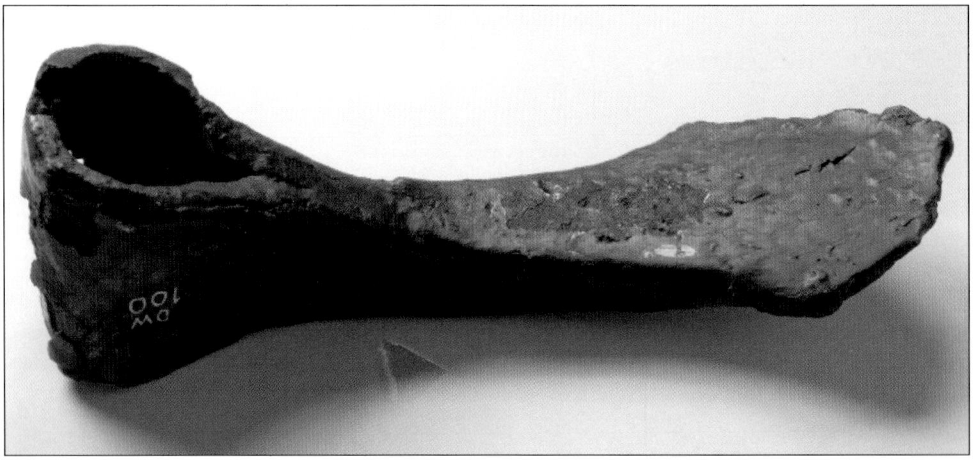

An Iron Age blade for a hoe from Blackburn Mill, Cockburnspath Berwickshire 80-200 AD.

(National Museums Scotland. Licensor www.scran.ac.uk)

Dunblane will have been very much affected by this intensified agriculture. With the new iron ploughs it will have been possible to plough virtually all the land in the parish even on high ground like Sheriffmuir. Any remaining forest will have been cleared. Agricultural historians have argued that the tools introduced in this period with access to iron were not significantly improved until the Agricultural Revolution in the late 18th century. As a result it is likely that the land in Dunblane about 250 BC will have taken on the appearance it had in the Middle Ages and the Early Modern period. Thus the mixed farming, crops, mainly oats with a little barley, and small numbers of horses, cows and sheep per settlement, evident in the many farm inventories of Dunblane inhabitants surviving from the 16th and 17th centuries may have emerged as early as the Iron Age. It is likely also that the main farming settlements in the parish, for example the Feddals, the Cambushinnies, the Auchinlays, the Corscaplies and the Quoiggs appeared in this period though the names are from a later date.

The changes in agriculture were matched by an explosion of building. The principal type of dwelling common throughout the country was the round house, a large and sophisticated building up to 18 metres in diameter, covering the same area as a medium sized modern bungalow. Its entrance was impressive with large swing doors. The outer walls were built of stone interlaced with timber and together with an inner ring of posts supported a huge conical thatched roof. The humans probably occupied a timber first floor divided into a series of cells and galleries that created a sophisticated living area. It is likely that as many as 20 individuals occupied a round house comprising at least an extended family. The central

Reconstruction of an Iron Age Hut by Archaeolink.
(Robert Gordon University. Licensor www.scran.ac.uk)

part of the ground floor was used for storing hay while the outer part round the walls was occupied by cattle during the winter months.

At Easterton between the Kilbryde and Argaty roads the probable site of a round house was excavated recently and is described by Lorna Main in her book *First Generations.* An enclosure appropriate to a round house was discovered measuring 46 by 49 metres. Unfortunately there was no trace of the round house itself because it had been destroyed by ploughing. It is likely that in the Iron Age there were a large number of round houses in Dunblane each at the centre of a significant farm settlement.

Brochs

From the round house emerged a structure that is unique to Scotland – the broch. The outer frame of this unusual tower-like building was made up of two dry-stone concentric walls which tapered towards the top and had a narrow gap between them. Galleries were created at different levels between the walls and were joined by a stone staircase. The enclosed part of the building was divided into a number of floors which opened off its inner walls and were constructed of timber. It is likely that the ground floor was used for animals and indoor farming activities while the two or more upper floors were occupied by humans. It used to be thought that brochs were confined to Orkney and Shetland and the north east of Scotland but recently a number have been discovered in the central belt of the country.

Broch Mousa is the best preserved broch in Scotland. The double walls are clear from the illustration – originally it would have been surrounded by much smaller houses the homes of the dependants of the owner of the broch.

(Historic Scotland. Licensor www.scran.ac.uk)

Archaeologists have found brochs very interesting. There is no doubt that they emerged about 400 BC in Orkney and Shetland extending to central and southern Scotland by the first century AD. Close to Dunblane in the Forth Valley five brochs have been discovered, the ones at Leckie and at Buchlyvie being thoroughly excavated. Perhaps surprisingly both have proved to be very rich in goods, the broch at Leckie producing over 2000 artefacts. Especially impressive has been the quality of the Roman goods discovered including high class Roman pottery and glass.

The origin and purpose of the brochs has puzzled archaeologists. It has been suggested that they were set up by a migrating elite from the north of Scotland which would account for the transmission of the considerable skills associated with their building. Recently this view has lost ground to the perfectly plausible hypothesis that the brochs in southern and central Scotland were built by important local people who have been described as "Iron Age lairds". The brochs appear to be well placed to dominate an area of agricultural land and its inhabitants as well as being large working farms. If any migration was necessary it is likely that the masons with the appropriate skills came from the north of Scotland. The quality of the Roman goods found in the brochs of central and southern Scotland has led to the suggestion that the brochs were distribution centres for high class Roman goods in the years before the building of the Antonine Wall. Once the Wall was constructed interaction with the Romans in central and southern Scotland would be direct and no intermediaries would be needed.

Fragments of Roman glass and pottery found at Fairy Knowe broch, Buchlyvie.

(by kind permission of Lorna Main)

CHAPTER 4

THE ROMAN INTERLUDE - INVADERS, OCCUPIERS AND NEIGHBOURS 79 - 410 AD

The Roman Army

In a book of this nature it is not appropriate to give a full description of the Roman army but it is important to emphasise how well organised and effective it was, far ahead of any force which the Caledonians, or any combination of northern tribes, could put into the field. At the time of Agricola's invasion of Scotland north of the Forth, the Roman army numbered about a quarter of a million men spread across the Empire. The core of the force was approximately 35 legions, each of 5,500 heavily armed infantry. The remainder of the army was made up of auxiliaries, infantry and cavalry in units of 1000 or fewer, men. The basic unit in a legion was a century, oddly between 80 and 90 men commanded by a centurion and in an auxiliary unit a troop of 32 men under a decurion. Both legionaries and auxiliaries served 25 years with the colours, conditions being so good that their expectation of life during their service was longer than comparable civilians.

A reconstruction by the Ermine Street Guard of a Roman soldier in full battle order.
(National Museums Scotland. Licensor www.scran.ac.uk)

Centurions and decurions could stay in the army as long as they liked – the record for a centurion established by archaeologists being an unbelievable 61 years. Soldiers were paid three times annually with deductions for food and equipment though on demobilisation the payments for equipment were refunded. Records of service and pay were maintained to a standard similar to our army 150 years ago. Training was rigorous, including route marches, drill, parades, weapon training and mock sieges.

The impressive organisation and formidable power of the Roman army can be seen by how it advanced into hostile territory. Josephus, formerly a general in the Jewish army and an eyewitness of the Roman campaign against the Jews from 66 to 70 AD, is the only person to describe in detail a Roman army on the march. The aim of the Romans was to establish a firm hold on hostile territory and to overawe the enemy. It is likely that the advances of the Roman army north of the Forth – of Agricola 79 AD, of Antoninus Pius' army c 140 AD and of Septimius Severus c 208/209 AD took this form. Given that Dunblane lies astride the best route into the north of Scotland it is likely that the Iron Age people living in and around Dunblane will have witnessed these advances albeit from the safety of the Trossachs and the Ochils. The order of march which extended as much as 20 miles was as follows:

Auxiliary infantry and archers scouting ahead to spot ambushes
A troop of legionaries and cavalry to provide a quick response
Ten men from each century to mark out the camp
A group of men equipped to clear the road
The Emperor's or army commander's baggage
The Emperor or army commander with his personal bodyguard
The cavalry of the legions
The siege train
The commanding officers and senior officers of the legions guarded by picked troops
The legionaries marching six abreast with their standards in front
The auxiliary units
The rearguard of infantry and cavalry

The ground covered each day was surprisingly limited, generally only twelve miles because the Romans were concerned with their security when they camped at night. As a result the march had to end well before dark so that an appropriate camp site could be chosen. It had to be defensible, have running water, and clear views of the surrounding ground. Above all a ditch had to be dug around the camp and a rampart erected from the loose soil surmounted by a row of stakes each man completing a section of the work.

A computer generated impression of a typical Roman marching camp in Scotland.
(National Museums Scotland. Licensor www.scran.ac.uk)

The elaborate nature even of an overnight camp means that many of them can still be located provided building has not taken place on the site. Aerial photography during World War Two and since, has revealed at least

70 marching camps in Scotland even if they were not evident at ground level. Most of the temporary camps were designed for units much smaller than an army, sometimes as little as an auxiliary force of 500 men. Presumably these smaller camps were erected by units moving up to reinforce or supply the main force.

Roman campaigns in Scotland 79 AD - 210 AD

It is also important to give a brief account of the three Roman campaigns in Scotland to provide a context for explaining the activities of the Romans in and around Dunblane.

First there was Agricola's campaign north of the Forth beginning in 79 AD culminating in the Battle of Mons Graupius in 83 AD which many believe was close to Inverness. During Agricola's campaign the dominant tribe between the Forth and the Tay were the Damnonii. After Mons Graupius Agricola was recalled almost immediately but evidence from the continuing construction of the legionary fortress at Inchtuthill twenty miles north of the Tay shows that the Romans intended staying permanently in the north of Scotland. However an emergency on the Danube led to the withdrawal of a legion from Scotland in the mid 80s AD and to judge by the evidence of coins surviving at Inchtuthill the whole force withdrew either in 86 or 87 AD.

A striking portrayal of the Emperor Antoninus Pius on a Roman coin, an Imperial Gold Aureus.

(Hunterian Museum and Art Gallery. Licensor www.scran.ac.uk)

The second campaign saw the construction of an earth rampart along the Forth-Clyde isthmus in 141-142 AD and known since then as the Antonine Wall. This advance from Hadrian's Wall was ordered by the Emperor Antoninus Pius who wanted to have a military triumph to his credit. It is likely that a campaign north of the Forth preceded the building of the wall and the Romans maintained a number of permanent garrisons between the Forth and the Tay during the life of the Wall, one of which was at Ardoch in Braco. The Antonine Wall was abandoned during the early 160s AD.

The third campaign was conducted by the Emperor Septimius Severus in person between 208 and 210 AD in response to incursions by the Caledonians the main tribe north of the Tay and the Miathi who were probably the dominant tribe in Fife and Central Scotland. It is likely that the Emperor's activities were north of the Forth extending well beyond the Tay to judge by the extensive building at the Roman bases at Cramond on the Forth and Carpow on the Tay. Septimius died at York in February 211 and his two sons withdrew after making treaties with the tribes north of the Forth which secured peace until 300 AD.

Roman marching camps in Dunblane

Three marching camps have been discovered in Dunblane, one on the ridge close to Keir House and two on Hillside. The camp on the ridge overlooking Dunblane is just to the east of Craigarnhall Farm. It was discovered by aerial photography in the late 1960s and was confirmed through excavation by Professor St Joseph in 1971 who estimated that it was constructed during Agricola's campaign of 79 - 83 AD. It was a 60 acre camp which is large enough according to Nic Fields in his recent book *Rome's Northern Frontier 70 - 235* to accommodate 11,000 men or the equivalent of two legions so it may have been occupied during an advance by a substantial part of Agricola's army. Sited spectacularly it has views extending to the Campsies on the south, the Ochils to the east, the Trossachs to the west and the Perthshire hills to the north. The excavation established that at least two of the camp entrances were guarded by a titulus that is a short piece of rampart and ditch placed a few feet in front of the entrances to the camp to prevent or break an enemy charge. The camp also has a three acre extension which may have been used to park the army's baggage train.

Crop marks showing the rampart of the Roman marching camp at Grassy Walls near Scone. The gate to the camp and the protecting titulus are indicated by arrows.
(Colin J.M. Martin. Licensor www.scran.co.uk)

The two other Roman camps in Dunblane are at Hillside. They were discovered by aerial photography in 1945 and today are largely covered by modern housing. The larger camp which also probably dates to Agricola's invasion is approximately 30 acres in size and could accommodate a sizeable auxiliary force or a legion. The smaller camp of about 20 acres lies inside the larger camp along part of its western defences and appears to have been constructed shortly after the larger camp. Excavations were conducted by Professor Annie Robertson in 1966 and 1967, single-handedly, according to the factor of the Keir estate before the new houses could be built. She did not find any artefacts but she did establish that large stretches of the ditches of the bigger camp had been cut from rock. The labour involved has led to speculation that the camp may have been designed to be occupied for a substantial period and not just for one night.

The siting of these two camps is also a surprise. Looking at them from below you wonder why they were placed under the crest of the hill. It is only when you climb up to Hillside Farm and stand on the part of the camp not occupied by housing that you realise how superbly sited they were. From there you can see all the neighbouring ranges of hills. It is likely that both of these camps were built and used by troops going forward and backward to support the main army up ahead.

At this point I had planned to include the photograph taken by the RAF in 1945 from which the two camps at Hillside were identified. In his *Portrait of Dunblane 1875-1975* published in 1980 Archie McKerracher used the image as the first illustration of his book. Unfortunately when I applied to The Committee for Aerial Photography at Cambridge University who hold the copyright of the image I was told that the Committee for the time being is not conducting any business so I would not be able to access the photograph.

It is intriguing that today we are able to walk across the sites of these camps constructed over 1900 years ago, possibly only occupied for one night and yet we can know approximately what was happening in each part of them. This is because the Romans were very systematic and laid out every camp in a broadly similar way. It was usually defended by a v-shaped ditch generally a metre deep and a metre wide. With the spoil from the ditch a rampart was constructed topped by timber stakes sharpened at both ends. Each soldier carried two of these stakes as part of his equipment. The camp was laid out with four gates and two roads running through it, one of these roads was the main road or *via principia*. In the centre was the head-quarters where the standards and administrative records of the unit were stored. Alongside were the sleeping quarters of the commanding officer and his officers and the hospital. The rest of the camp was taken up by the tents of the soldiers in long lines with space for the storage of food and equipment. Each tent was three metres square and housed 8 men. Soldiers were chosen to man the guard during the night with the penalty for going to sleep being death.

Dunblane and the Roman road north of the River Forth

Though the three Roman camps in Dunblane are of great interest, of even more significance is the strategic importance of Dunblane and the area immediately to its north for the Roman campaigns in Scotland, especially that of Agricola. Thus the only Roman road north of the Forth and, aside from the sea, its only artery for communications, supply and reinforcement ran through Dunblane. Roman roads were made to last with a bottom layer of large stones, reinforced by smaller stones and topped by gravel and sand, all pressed firmly into place. They ranged from 10 to 4 metres wide. The Roman road north of the Forth has been established from just north of Camelon to the King's Knot in Stirling then according to the Ordinance Survey Map of Roman Britain it resumes just south of Glenbank Farm close to the Little Chef on the A9 beyond Dunblane. From there it runs to Greenloaning, Ardoch and along the Gask Ridge to the River Tay at Carpow *(see the map over).*

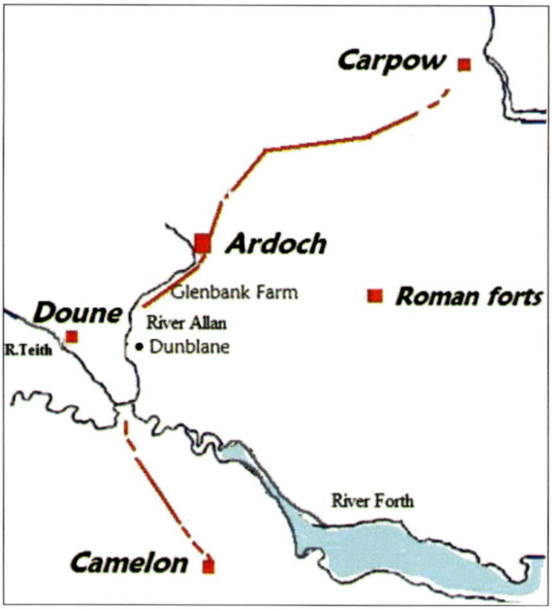

The Roman road from Camelon to Carpow on the River Tay.

The missing stretch of the road from Stirling to Glenbank is obviously of great interest to people living in Dunblane and its surroundings and its possible route has led to much debate.

The first area of controversy is to establish where the Roman road crossed the River Forth. D.J.Woolliscroft and B. Hoffmann in their recent book *Rome's First Frontier* provide the most up to date and convincing assessment of the alternatives. They argue that there are three crossing points that would have been particularly favoured by the Romans. They point out that evidence for the road ends at the King's Knot heading west of the Castle Rock. If that line were followed directly they argue that the crossing would have been at Kildean Hospital. Alternatively in their view the road could have continued along the Forth to cross at the Fords of Frew, the favoured crossing of the Forth in the Middle Ages. They also consider it possible that the road could have turned from the Kings Knot to cross near the old Stirling Bridge.

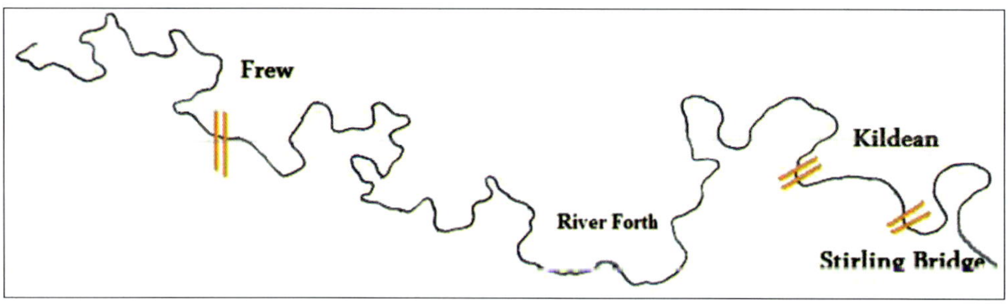

Possible crossing points of the Roman road on the River Forth.

The second area of controversy concerns the line followed by the road from the Forth to just south of Glenbank. Did it go on a rather circuitous route via the small Roman fort at Doune or directly up the Carse, east of Keir, following the present M9 and then through what is modern Dunblane to Glenbank? Woolliscroft and Hoffmann argue that at present no definitive answer can be given to this question. They state that the line of the Roman road probably resumes just east of Kinbuck on the edge of a disused quarry at Glassingall heading north east (see the map below). If the line of the road is traced back from the quarry they argue that it could either lead to crossing the River Allan and heading for Doune or following the route of the B8033 towards Dunblane and then presumably directly to the Forth. In their view it is not possible on the available evidence to decide whether the road went directly through Dunblane or via Doune.

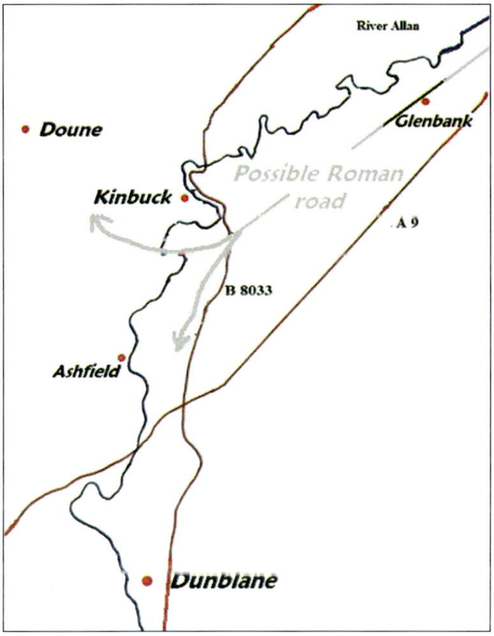

Possible routes of the Roman road from the Forth to Glenbank.

Dunblane and Rome's "First Frontier" 79 - 86 AD

During Agricola's campaign this road which was so vital to the Romans became of even greater significance because a frontier was created along it, which has been described by Woolliscroft and Hoffmann as *Rome's First Frontier*. As such it is the pre-cursor of other Roman frontiers on the Rhine, on the Danube, as well as that dividing Britain along Hadrian's Wall and then the Antonine Wall.

This "First Frontier" was formed by a series of forts and watch towers less than a mile apart running beside the Roman road north of the Forth. As is evident from the map below these forts and signal stations have been discovered in numbers along the Gask Ridge, on the approaches to Ardoch and petering out with the signal station at Greenloaning and a mile further south the fort at Glenbank, both in modern Dunblane. It is reasonable to presume that the frontier continued along the lost road through Dunblane and at least as far as the Forth. There are two other characteristics of the frontier which are clear from the map. Out to the west some 20 to 30 miles from the main line are five forts apparently guarding the entry to significant Highland glens. Then north of the Tay is the Roman legionary fortress of Inchtuthill acting as a hinge between the western forts and the line of forts and watch towers. Construction of Inchtuthill began in the mid eighties after the battle of Mons Graupius and was abandoned before completion when reinforcements were required on the Danube frontier in 86 or 87AD.

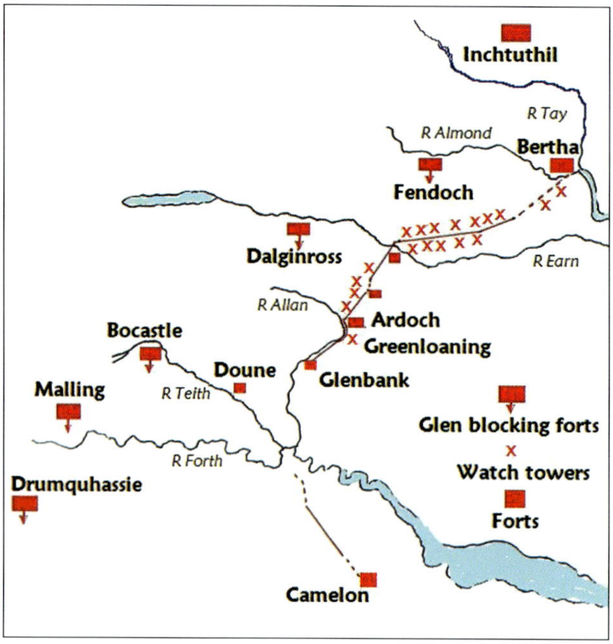

Map of Rome's "First Frontier".

Woolliscroft and Hoffmann have suggested a number of reasons for the building of this frontier. First they have argued that the frontier was largely defensive and aimed at preventing a successful attack from the Highlands. In this connection with its north-south axis it appears to be positioned to protect Fife which was a rich corn producing area. It even has been suggested that the absence of Roman camps in Fife shows that the tribe occupying the region were allies of the Romans. Before invading a territory it was common for the Romans to make alliances with some of the native tribes to make the task of conquest easier. Second and equally likely the frontier could have been used as a base for further advance into the north of Scotland. After all it faced the Highlands and was clearly designed to secure the only Roman road north of the Forth their sole line of communication and supply aside from the sea. Thirdly it has been suggested that like Hadrian's Wall this first Roman frontier may have been designed to control the movement of native peoples in the area and even their economic activity through a customs barrier.

This "First Frontier" is of course very different from Hadrian's Wall and the Antonine Wall being porous as opposed to being a continual wall or palisade. It was made up mainly of watch towers and fortlets, the towers being manned by as few as 8 men and the fortlets by only ten times that number. Occasionally there is a bigger fort as at the mouth of the glens to the west and at Camelon, Ardoch, Strageath and Bertha in the main line but even these forts did not hold more than an auxiliary unit of at the most 500 men. As a result any sizeable enemy force would have been able to penetrate the defensive system very easily. However they would have been observed from the start and news of their gathering passed very quickly down the line of watch towers and forts to the Forth or the Tay allowing an army to be gathered quickly to meet the invaders.

It is likely, then, that the line of forts that apparently ends at Glenbank in Dunblane continued either on a straight line to the Forth or by a loop through the fort at Doune. So given that the Roman forts and watch towers on this first frontier were less than a mile apart there will, as Woolliscroft and Hoffman have pointed out recently, be other watch towers and possibly fortlets in Dunblane remaining to be discovered. They state that the discovery of these additional sites is hampered by the nature of the land south of Glenbank which is pastoral not arable and therefore will not yield so readily to aerial photography the tell tale crop marks of a Roman fortification. However if you continue south from the fort at Glenbank along the known line of the Roman road and assume the same gap between other watch towers and fortlets on the line the next fortification would be close to Balhaldie. The possibility that the Roman road ran through Dunblane, which has not been discounted by Woolliscroft and Hoffman, raises the intriguing possibility that there was a Roman watch tower on the top of Holmhill. The views from there are so superb to the south and north that it is difficult to imagine the Romans ignoring such an obvious site.

Before leaving Rome's "First Frontier" it is important to describe what has been discovered at the sites of the Roman watch tower at Greenloaning and the fortlet at Glenbank.

A drawing reconstructing the Roman watch tower at Muir o'Fauld on the Gask Ridge.

(Historic Scotland. Licensor www.scran.ac.uk)

The postholes denoting a watch tower at Greenloaning were discovered from the air by RCAHMS in 1986 and the site was excavated by Woolliscroft and Hoffmann in 1995. It stands about 11 metres from the Roman road and has an excellent view to Ardoch in the north and Glenbank in the south. The tower, entirely of timber was supported by four big posts and is the largest Roman tower of its kind ever found. It was defended by a ring of two ditches which perhaps surprisingly were only 18 inches deep implying that the Romans did not anticipate a serious threat from the local tribes. It appears that there were two building phases the initial erection of the tower followed by demolition and re-erection very soon after the demolition. When the site was finally abandoned the tower was demolished, the posts removed and everything else systematically burnt. No significant artefacts e.g. coins were found on the site except for two small scraps of coarse pottery which were not dateable. There is no evidence of the watch tower on the ground today.

The fort at Glenbank designed for a force of 80 men and very similar to the fort at Kaims was discovered by aerial photography in 1983 and has been excavated twice most recently by Woolliscroft and Hoffmann. It had two ditches with a turf rampart and a single entrance close to the road north protected by a tower resting on four posts. Surprisingly there is no evidence of buildings inside the fort. It is possible that they were never constructed or that they were of a kind that has left no trace. Another possibility is that the troops were sent out from a neighbouring fort and lived in tents while garrisoning the fortlet. There were no artefacts discovered at the site and nothing visible at ground level though the fort was almost certainly constructed in the first century AD.

The Roman fort at Ardoch

The building of the Roman road north, the defensive barrier along it and the dating of the marching camps in Dunblane to the Agricolan campaign means that all the evidence of Roman activity in Dunblane is focused on their first campaign in Scotland. It is likely however that some of the sites especially the marching camps will have been re-used in later campaigns. Thus archaeologists are convinced that the spectacular Roman camp at Ardoch, one of at least four on the site, was occupied during the Agricolan campaign 79 to 83 AD and during the years when the Antonine Wall was garrisoned 142 to c 160 AD. It has six huge ditches to the east and north, at least 2.5 metres deep and 6 metres wide, the best preserved defences of any Roman camp in Britain.

The Roman fort at Ardoch in Braco.
(RCAHMS. Licensor www.scran.ac.uk)

The excavations of the 1890s demonstrated that at least one and possibly all of the gates were massively defended by huge wooden towers. During the second period of Roman occupation the fort was one of three north of the Antonine Wall, the other two being at Strageath, just north of Ardoch, and at Bertha on the Tay. Their probable purpose was to monitor any gathering of hostile forces north of the Wall by scouting and other means and report back to the troops on the Wall. The garrison of the fort appears to have been a unit of auxiliary cavalry which is appropriate in the circumstances. The presence of such a unit at least in the first period of occupation of the fort was proved by discovery of a tombstone during the excavations of the 1890s. It recorded the death of Ammonius a centurion of the First Cohort of Spanish Auxiliaries who had served for 27 years. The inscription translates as follows:

"To the shade of the late Ammonius son of Damio a centurion of the first cohort of Spaniards who served for 27 years. His heirs set this up."

Relations between the Roman army and the natives 79 AD - 165 AD

Everybody reading this account will wonder what type of interaction took place between the native population, especially around Dunblane, and the Roman army in its forays into Scotland. A lot depended on whether or not a tribe was an ally of the Romans. Initially the local people in the path of the Roman army will undoubtedly have fled to the hills. Quickly however more normal relations will have developed as any fighting ceased or moved further north as the campaign progressed. The Roman army lived mainly off the land so they will have needed extensive supplies of food, building materials and commodities like leather for shoes and military equipment. They either bought these commodities from the natives or they forced the local tribes to pay a tribute in goods they required.

There is plentiful evidence of voluntary local trade between the Romans and the native population in Central Scotland. Already the thriving trade in Roman luxury goods apparently centred on brochs along the Forth has been noted. There are also the annexes which grew up alongside the Roman forts along the Antonine Wall. For example excavations at Inveresk in the 1960s showed that there was a wide range of services ranging from tanning to prostitution in its annexe. More recently Woolliscroft and Hoffmann have drawn attention to the close proximity of many of the round houses of local people to Roman fortifications north of the Forth and to intensified farming activity coinciding with the Roman presence to judge by the pollen analysis in the ditches of Roman installations.

Evidence of forced tribute and taxes comes from the speech which Tacitus puts into the mouth of Calgacus, the leader of the Caledonians, before the battle of Mons Graupius. There Calgacus complains that the Romans had levied tribute on the local population, requisitioning their corn, forcing them to labour on the roads and conscripting them for a range of tasks. Of course it is very unlikely that Calgacus made any sort of speech even to the assembled tribal chiefs and even less likely that a transcript of the speech had reached Tacitus. He was clearly writing for effect in his eulogy of Agricola but the Romans did raise tribute from conquered peoples and Tacitus may be reporting what the Romans did in Scotland north of the Forth.

Living beside the Romans after their withdrawal from the Antonine Wall c 165 AD

It is perhaps surprising how little the mighty Roman Empire appeared to influence the life of the tribes in Scotland after their withdrawal c 165 AD.

There is quite a lot of evidence of trade but it appears to have been limited mainly to luxury goods for the tribal aristocracy of Scotland. Apart from places like Traprain Law and the brochs Roman goods are found but not in profusion and are generally of low quality. It appears that the principal influence of the Romans was on the life style of the chieftains and their aristocracy especially their dining habits.

In other spheres the Romans had little influence. For example they appear to have had no impact on native agriculture in Scotland with all the developments that are traceable to the Iron Age preceding their arrival. Indeed it has recently been argued that some of the farm implements in use in Scotland at this time, for example querns, were superior to those employed by the Romans. Nor was any attempt made by the people living north of the Tweed to imitate Roman styles of building, or artistic designs, or urban settlement during these years.

A fragment of Samian tableware from a broch in Caithness.

(National Museums Scotland Licensor www.scran.ac.uk)

There is however one area in which the Romans may have had an indirect but significant impact on life in Scotland at this time, that is its political development. Such a change will have been important for the people living in the area in and around modern Dunblane.

At the time when the Romans arrived in Britain it appears that the tribes of southern England were more advanced than those occupying Scotland. The former had kings, proto urban settlements and coinage. Tribes in Scotland had apparently none of these features. No kings are mentioned in Tacitus' account of Agricola's campaigns in Scotland and when a leader does emerge at Mons Graupius, Calgacus, he is chosen for his military prowess not because he is a tribal leader.

There are signs that this situation had altered significantly by the time the Romans abandoned Britain in 410 AD. This change was brought about partly by the policy adopted by the Romans to the tribes beyond their frontiers and partly by the reaction of the tribes to the Romans and their policy.

It is now accepted by historians like James Fraser in his recent book *From Caledonia to Pictland Scotland to 795* that the Romans adopted a distinctive policy to the tribes beyond their frontiers. They wanted to ensure that these tribes remained peaceful and did not invade the Roman Empire. As a result they made every effort to have particular allies across a frontier and to get on well even with those tribes with whom they did not have a special relationship.

It is likely that the Romans had a strong alliance with the Votadini who occupied what is modern Lothian. This relationship is suggested by the absence of Roman camps in this territory despite the Romans campaigning in Scotland on and off from 79 to 210 AD. It may also be indicated by the superb quality of Roman goods found at Traprain Law which has been described as the Acropolis of the Votadini. A similar special relationship may have existed closer to Dunblane with a surprising absence of Roman camps throughout Fife implying that the tribe living there were allies of the Romans.

But the other tribes in Scotland including the Miathi who dominated the territory between the Forth and the Tay including Dunblane were not neglected. With them the Romans adopted the policy of the carrot and the stick. To keep them quiet they gave the tribal leaders lavish presents of Roman jewellery, tableware and coinage. Over 70 such hoards have been discovered north of the Forth, the nearest one to Dunblane being at Falkirk. If for a period this policy broke down and the tribes crossed Hadrian's Wall in force a savage punitive expedition was mounted laying waste to large areas of tribal territory. The actions of the Emperor, Septimius Severus and his sons 208 - 210 AD in response to the Caledonian and Miathi incursion of 196 in which a Roman general was killed provides an excellent example of this policy in action. The Emperor launched a punitive campaign extending beyond the Tay and after his death at York in 211 his sons made a peace with the tribes presumably sweetened by many gifts. It was a peace that lasted for nearly a century.

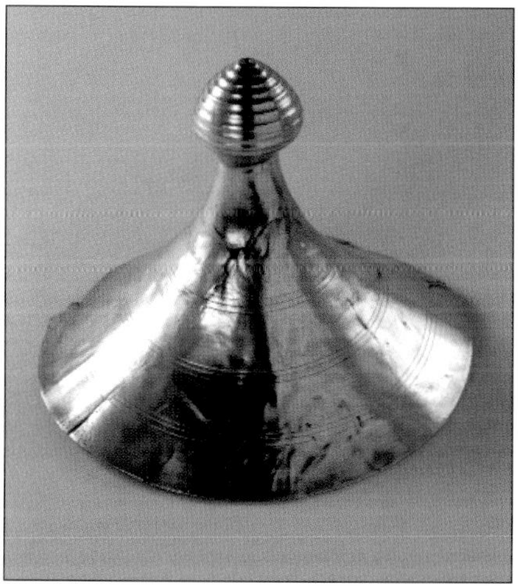

The most famous example of Roman treasure trove is from Traprain Law in East Lothian. Above is a silver cover, one of 150 items in the horde. The treasure was buried early in the 5th century and is probably a gift from the Romans to the Votadini.

(National Museums Scotland. Licensor www.scran.ac.uk)

The reaction of the tribes north of the Forth to the policy adopted by the Romans is also important. It is likely that the tribal elite admired the Romans and to enhance their authority adopted as far as possible the lifestyle of the Romans. Hence their acceptance of lavish Roman gifts and their involvement in the trade with north western Europe that would provide a regular supply of these goods. At the same time pressure by the Romans on these tribes north of the Forth appears to have united them and increased their strength. Their growth in power can be seen in the events of 367-370 when the Picts (presumably including the Miathi), Gaels and Saxons invaded Roman Britain and even though they were eventually driven back their incursions signalled the end of the Roman Empire on the British Isles. The alliance of the Picts with the Gaels from Ireland and the Saxons from Europe revealed an unprecedented diplomatic maturity. The devastating nature of the attack showed that the military capacity of the Picts had increased most likely with a formidable war band or cohort at the centre of their host. Also the structure of their states had matured from the time of Agricola when it took two or three campaigning seasons by the Romans for a native leader to emerge. Finally it is worth noting that from the 1st to the 4th century there appears to have been a coalescence of the tribes north of the Forth from the twelve tribes named by Ptolemy to the two tribes identified by Ammianus Marcellanus in the late 4th century both of them described as Picts.

CHAPTER 5

THE DARK AGES IN SCOTLAND AND DUNBLANE 410 - 1000 AD

So far what was happening in the area now occupied by Dunblane and its immediate vicinity has been described but of course there was no town and probably not even a hamlet here during these thousands of years. This was typical of Scotland as a whole where aside from two sites in the Lothians, Edinburgh Castle and Traprain Law and in Roxburghshire, Eildon Hill there is no evidence of towns or even large villages let alone named sites with the names coming down to us. After 400 AD the first settlements that are named on our maps today began to emerge, among them Dunblane making it one of the oldest places in Scotland. Since the foundation of Dunblane is associated with St Blane who probably lived in the early 7th century it is clearly related to the spread of Christianity. As a result in describing the Dark Ages in Scotland and Dunblane it is necessary to focus on the religion of the period and to map out briefly the political structure of the country since rulers were crucial to religious development in the Dark Ages.

The Struggle for the Control of Scotland and the part played by Central Scotland and Dunblane in that conflict 410 - 1000 AD

The main powers in Scotland 410 - 600 AD

Map showing the main kingdoms in Scotland between 400 and 600 AD.

There were five significant powers in Scotland in the two centuries following the departure of the Romans from Britain. Little is known about conditions in the west and south west of Lowland Scotland and elsewhere our knowledge of events in the country is sketchy. However in his book mentioned above James Fraser has made excellent use of the limited evidence available.

To the south on either side of Hadrian's Wall there were two states – Bernicia to the north centring on Bamburgh and to the south Deira on York – which were to have a significant impact on Scottish History in the coming centuries. After much conflict these two states were to unite uneasily as the Kingdom of Northumbria. Over the last 20 years historians have suggested a number of explanations of the origins of Bernicia and Deira, from being descendants of German soldiers who served on Hadrian's Wall to being Anglo-Saxon mercenaries invited over to defend Britain after the Roman army had left.

Further north and centred on the Lothians was the romantically named kingdom of Gododdin. The people of Gododdin were almost certainly descendants of the Votadini who had probably been the allies of the Romans with their capital at Traprain Law. Traprain Law was abandoned after the Romans withdrew from Britain and Edinburgh Castle then became the new capital of the kingdom.

To the far west of Scotland was Dal Riata, centring on Argyll, Kintyre and the islands off shore. In Dal Riata there were five small kingdoms or as James Fraser describes them five principal kindreds or tribes. From time to time vicious conflict broke out between these kingdoms or kindreds with a dominant king emerging. Dal Riata is clearly a significant area since it includes Iona and for those interested in Dunblane Kingarth on the Isle of Bute which was St Blane's base. Thirty years ago it was accepted that Dal Riata was dominated by the Scots, a tribe who had invaded or migrated from Ireland in the 4th and 5th centuries. That view is now discounted since there is no archaeological evidence to support it. Rather, given the geographical position of Dal Riata, facing Ireland to the west and very close to that country by sea and cut off from the rest of Scotland by mountain ranges, it is accepted that Dal Riata shared a common culture and language with Ireland especially with the north of that country with movements of population either way from time to time.

The hill of Dunadd in Mid-Argyll on which was established what may have been the main fortress of the High Kings of Dal Riata.
(RCAHMS. Licensor www.scran.ac.uk)

To the north were the Picts, extending from the Tay to the Moray Firth and Inverness and possibly further. It has been suggested that Pictland was divided into a number of kingdoms with a High King. Also the view of the Romans that there were northern and southern Picts with the Grampians forming the dividing line between them has been generally accepted.

Finally and most important for the history of Dunblane is the British Kingdom of Alt Clut or of the Miathi. It has been suggested that the Damnonii, the tribe dominating Central Scotland at the time of Agricola's invasion of Scotland north of the Forth in 79 AD, had been replaced by the Miathi by the late 2nd century AD when together with the Caledonii, later the Picts, they invaded Roman Britain and faced retaliation by Septimius Severus. This kingdom appears to have been centred around the Clyde at Dumbarton Rock and controlled Clydesdale as well as the territory between the Forth and the Tay including of course Dunblane.

There are two important documentary references to this Kingdom of Alt Clut or of the Miathi between 400 and 600 at a time when documentary references to events in Scotland are very rare. In the mid 5th century St Patrick wrote a furious letter to Coroticus, a king whose capital was at Dumbarton Rock, presumably the King of Alt Clut. He protested to the King that Irishmen whom St Patrick had himself converted to Christianity had been enslaved by followers of King Coroticus, men who themselves were at least nominally Christians. In so doing Patrick who was a Briton refers to the followers of Coroticus as "my own people" and as "fellow citizens". In other words Coroticus was King of a British Kingdom. The Miathi also figured in *Adomnan's Vita Columbae, Life of Columba.* Adomnan's book was written in the late 7th century but describes Columba's activities as abbot of Iona between 563 and his death in 597. Adomnan relates how Columba went on a mission to convert the Miathi. So Dunblane between 400 and 600 was part of a British Kingdom in Central Scotland which will be of significance when we come to consider the origins of Dunblane.

Aerial view of the Fortress of Alt Clut, literally Clyde Rock, capital of the Kingdom of Strathclyde

(Crown Copyright, reproduced by courtesy of Historic Scotland. Licensor www.scran.ac.uk)

Power struggles and the resulting political changes 410 - 700 AD

From 410 to 700 AD the main parts of Scotland to change hands were in the south east and centre of the country.

During this period the kingdom of Gododdin disappeared. There is a poem whose derivation is contested but which may be from the 6th century. It provides a description of a battle near Catterick between the warriors of Gododdin and a local army presumably from Deira and Bernicia.

In the battle the army of Gododdin is totally destroyed and the flower of its warriors all killed. Whatever the truth about this battle there is no doubt that in the first half of the 7th century the Bernicians and Deirans, or as they were increasingly called the Northumbrians, took the conflict into Gododdin. In 640 King Oswald of Northumbria is described as besieging and capturing Edinburgh probably the castle and by 655 Oswy, Oswald's brother had conquered all Gododdin and reached the Forth, possibly at Stirling.

The Kingdom of Alt Clut or the Miathi which included Dunblane also came under threat during this period. Aedan the first king from Dal Riata whose activities are recorded is described as campaigning north of the Forth in the early 580s eventually winning a victory either in 584 or 585 in a province called Manau. Clackmannan a place name clearly associated with Manau may have been the centre of this province. Whether Aedan was able to maintain his position is unclear but certainly by the middle of the next century Northumbria was campaigning between the Forth and the Tay. By 660 the Northumbrians had been so successful that they had wrested much of this territory from the Kingdom of Alt Clut setting up a client kingdom under Talorcan who was a nephew of King Oswy of Northumbria. The scene was set for a struggle between Northumbria and the Picts for the control not only of the land between the Forth and the Tay but for the rest of northern Scotland. Initially the Northumbrians were victorious at the battle of the Two Rivers in 671 but the decisive battle was at Nechtansmere in 685 where the Northumbrians suffered a massive defeat with their King, Ecgfrith, being killed. As a result by 700 the land between the Forth and the Tay including Dunblane had been absorbed into Pictland for good.

Section of the Pictish carved stone at Aberlemno which may depict the battle of Nechtansmere in which the Picts decisively defeated the Northumbrians. A Northumbrian soldier identified by his helmet is shown fleeing from the battlefield. Aberlemno is close to Dunnichen Hill which is thought to be the site of the battle. Both Aberlemno and Dunnichen Hill are a few miles either side of Forfar.

(Historic Scotland. Licensor www.scran.ac.uk)

Power struggles and the resulting political changes 700 - 1000 AD

The period from 700 to 1000 AD is dominated by the piratical raids and ultimately invasions by the Vikings which began in the 790s.

Prior to the arrival of the Vikings the Picts and the Northumbrians became the dominant powers in Scotland, the Picts to the north of the Forth and the Northumbrians to the south. It appears that Dal Riata was conquered during the years 734-741 by the Pictish king Onuist. As a result it disappears from the records for a generation, re-emerging as a subject kingdom of Pictland though with its own kings. The records also show that in 756 the lowland Kingdom of Alt Clut or of Strathclyde was extinguished by an attack mounted jointly from the combined armies of King Onuist of Pictland and King Eadberct of Northumbria. About this time and possibly as a result of the disappearance of the Kingdom of Alt Clut Northumbrian influence in the South West of Scotland and especially at Whithorn is evident.

The Viking invasions beginning in the late 8th century and intensifying during the 9th century had a significant impact on the power structure in the north and south of Scotland and this is the period when Dunblane is first mentioned in historical records. The Viking incursions started in the 790s with piratical raids on islands like Iona and Lindisfarne and exposed coastal regions of Scotland but apparently without any intention of permanent settlement. This situation was to change early in the 9th century. It is likely at this time that the Vikings conquered and began to settle the islands to the north and west of Scotland and they may have conquered most of Dal Riata. Then in 839 disaster hit northern Scotland when the Vikings won a massive victory over the Picts in which the kings of Pictland and Dal Riata were killed together with virtually all their warriors.

Photograph of a man dressed as a Viking warrior based on grave finds in Scandinavia.

(Multimedia Team - National Museums Scotland. Licensor www.scran.ac.uk)

This defeat had a number of consequences. First, and this was of great importance for Dunblane, it appears that the defeat and death of the King of the Picts by the Vikings in 839 led to the immediate re-emergence of the Kingdom of Alt Clut, or Strathclyde, as it was increasingly called from now on. As a result Dunblane has its first mention in historical records in the 9th or 10th century Chronicle of Scottish Kings. During an account of the reign of Kenneth MacAlpine it is reported that Dunblane was sacked by the Britons, presumably of Strathclyde, in 841. This report of course confirms that Dunblane was no longer in the Kingdom of Strathclyde but was now part of Pictland.

Second and this also may have a bearing on Dunblane, the defeat of the Picts by the Vikings in 839 led to Kenneth MacAlpine becoming King, first of Dal Riata in 839, and then of Pictland in 841. The traditional story of his accession is that as King of Dal Riata Kenneth MacAlpine destroyed the Picts and set up the kingdom of Alba. It is now accepted however that Kenneth MacAlpine succeeded to the throne of Pictland peacefully since he appears to have ruled the Kingdom for 16 years until his death without any evidence of serious internal dissent. Also far from the Picts disappearing from the records with the accession of Kenneth MacAlpine reference continued to them in documents until the end of the century.

Kenneth MacAlpine is also seen as introducing significant changes in Pictland. To revive the resistance of the Picts to the attacks of the Vikings he had the relics of St Columba, who according to Bede was already seen as the patron saint of Pictland, transported from Iona to Dunkeld. The Scottish historian, Alex Woolf, has recently suggested that it was at this time that the relics of St Blane's monastery on the Isle of Bute were moved to Dunblane. He argues that the reference to Dunblane being sacked by the Britons in 841 shows that already there was a strong association between the settlement and St Blane which may indicate that the relics of the saint had already been moved to Dunblane. Certainly throughout the Middle Ages Dunblane was the place where St Blane's relics were lodged and worshipped and the case for their transfer at the height of the Viking threat is persuasive.

19th century impression of the now lost seal of Dunkeld Cathedral dating to the 11th or 12th century. It shows the reliquary (box) that would have held St Columba's relics when they were transferred from Iona to Dunkeld on the order of King Kenneth MacAlpine in the 9th century. Above the reliquary is a drawing of Columba's crozier.

(Perth Museum and Art Gallery. Licensor www.scran.ac.uk)

From 900 AD to the early 1000s AD Viking pressure on Scotland continued. In the north of Scotland the Vikings seized and settled Shetland, Orkney, Caithness and nearly all the north western islands of Scotland. They also attacked Pictland frequently and in the lowlands destroyed Northumbria and in 870 captured Dumbarton the capital of the kingdom of Strathclyde. The severity of the assault can be gauged by the report that Dunblane may have been sacked by King Ronald of Denmark in 912 though it is not clear from the document whether Dunblane or Dublin is the town being laid waste.

All was not lost however. As in England out of the ashes of the Viking attacks there arose strong kingdoms which were eventually to unite each country. In Scotland the most successful kingdom in this period of uncertainty was the Kingdom of the Picts which by 900 AD was re-labelled the Kingdom of Alba thereby making what must have seemed the outrageous claim to be the Kings of Britain. From their base of the old southern Pictland the descendants of this dynasty eventually gained control of the Lothians capturing Edinburgh during the reign of the Pictish King Ildulb (954-962). It is interesting that Dunblane was part of the heartland from which Scotland as a united country was to emerge.

Christian Scotland 410 - 1000 AD – conversion, consolidation and the place of Dunblane in these processes

Conversion and consolidation up to 600 AD

The process by which Scotland was converted to Christianity has been reinterpreted radically in recent years. It used to be thought that St Ninian, St Columba and St Kentigern and of course St Blane came as missionaries to different parts of Scotland to convert the native population which was completely pagan. Hutchison Cockburn in his book *The Celtic Church in Dunblane* took this view. Rather fancifully he describes St Blane and his monks in 602 travelling from Kingarth on the Isle of Bute, up the Clyde valley, then along the Forth, and finally arriving at the site to be named after him where St Blane secured a grant of land from the local ruler and set up his monastery.

This view has been almost totally revised. Today historians consider that men like St Ninian, St Columba, St Kentigern and St Blane came to a country that was already largely Christian to consolidate the faith rather like St Augustine did at Canterbury. Recently Tom Clancy has even argued persuasively that textual confusion in the Middle Ages has led to St Ninian being wrongly identified as a British saint coming to south west Scotland in approximately 400 AD. Rather he argues that Ninian was actually a priest called Uinniau who came to Scotland about 550 AD from Ireland. In support of their argument that the country was Christian when the saints arrived historians point to Christian burials from the 400s AD for example the 'Latinus stone' in south west Scotland, the 'Cat Stane' at Edinburgh Airport and the fifth century cemetery on the Isle of May in the Forth which is very likely to be Christian. St Patrick's letter to Coroticus about 450 AD which has already been mentioned is also cited as evidence that Christianity was established in Central Scotland and probably in Pictland at this time. The argument is reinforced by the lives of St Columba and St Kentigern which have come down to us. For example Adomnan writing 80 or 90 years after Columba's death describes the saint as an ascetic spending nearly all his time at Iona as opposed to going on missionary journeys. Clearly a revision of this nature is significant for our view of St Blane.

How then was Scotland converted to Christianity? Today historians consider that Christianity was initially spread haphazardly in Roman Britain between 150 and 400 AD, and rather later in Scotland, by individuals such as soldiers returning from serving in the Roman army and traders moving from place to place. This process has been described by James Fraser as the bottom-up method of conversion. This form of conversion was supplemented by the top-down conversion in which a ruler was converted and his people followed suit. Of course many of the ruler's subjects may already have been Christian or have been familiar with its main themes. After the Emperor Constantine's espousal of Christianity in the early 4th century, and the adoption of Christianity by Rome, rulers outside the Empire will have seen conversion to Christianity as politically advantageous as well as evidence of being progressive and forward looking. Bede's description of King Edwin of Northumbria's conversion to Christianity in the early 7th century is a good example of this type of conversion. It is likely that the people living in and near modern Dunblane between 400 and 600 AD were converted through both these processes.

Even though they did not convert the people, men like St Columba played an important part in the consolidation of Christianity in Scotland. St Columba about whom we know a good deal because of Adomnan's biography came to Scotland in 563. He was from the family of the High Kings of Ireland and may have been involved in an attempt to overthrow one of his kin who occupied the throne coming to Scotland as a penance. Once arrived far from behaving like a missionary Columba spent much of his time at Iona as an example of the saintly monk and scholar. It was for these very virtues that Iona became world famous within a century of Columba's death. When he did leave Iona Columba interacted with kings rather than their peoples and it has been plausibly argued by James Fraser that his mission was to reform Scottish monasticism as opposed to converting the population to Christianity.

St Blane and the foundation of Dunblane early in the 7th century AD

We know very little about St Blane. A detailed account of St Blane's life and missionary work was published by James Hutchison Cockburn in his *The Celtic Church in Dunblane.* Unfortunately the largely mediaeval sources on which he and other historians drew at the time are no longer considered reliable by modern authorities because they were not nearly contemporary with the events described. In contrast Hutchison Cockburn's *Mediaeval Bishops of Dunblane* published in 1955 and on which I shall draw later in this book is still quoted by historians because his sources are contemporary with the events he describes.

What then do we know about St Blane that can be relied upon? Alex Woolf in the New Edinburgh History of Scotland *From Pictland to Alba* states the few bald facts of which we can be reasonably certain. St. Blane, spelt Blåån in the sources, was a Briton who lived in the 6th century and dwelt at the monastery of Kingarth on the Isle of Bute.

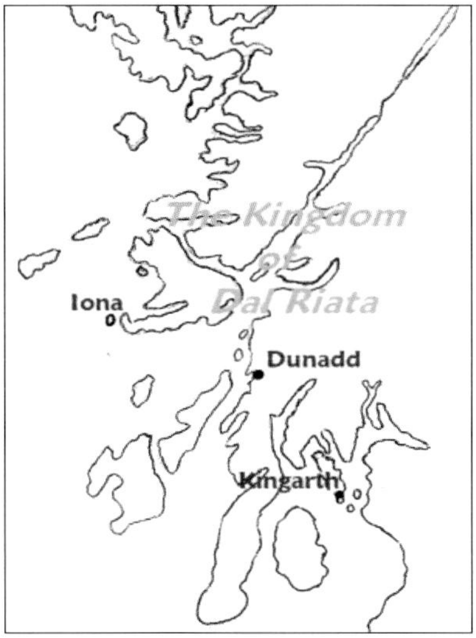

Map of Dal Riata showing the location of the monasteries at Iona and Kingarth.

What do we know about the monastery of Kingarth where St Blane was based? It is strongly associated with one of the kingdoms of Dal Riata, Cemel Comgaill. James Fraser in *From Caledonia to Pictland Scotland* suggests that Kingarth was the chief monastery of that kingdom since it was less than a kilometre from the possible royal centre at the hill fort of Little Donagail. James Fraser goes on to suggest that Kingarth may have been a very significant monastery even a rival to Iona. He attributes its modern obscurity and the fame of Iona partly to the fortuitous survival of evidence and partly to Iona's close association with Northumbria which may have arisen from the boy king Edwin spending some of his exile c 600 AD with the King of Cenn Gard on whose land Iona was based. Alex Woolf in his *From Pictland to Albu* also considers that Kingarth was a significant religious centre possibly the headquarters of the Bishops of Dal Riata in the middle of the 7th century.

The remains of the 12th century church dedicated to St Blane at Kingarth. There are some traces of the 6th century monastery where St Blane lived a well, several early crosses, part of the boundary wall and possible traces of monastic cells.
(RCAHMS. Licensor www.scran.ac.uk)

Even though we know very little about St Blane it is still important to speculate about his contact with Dunblane.

The Pictish standing stone found embedded in the walls of the Chapter House at the time of the restoration of the Cathedral.
(photograph by Len Bovill)

The traditional view of his relationship with the town is based on the derivation of the place-name Dunblane which over the ages has been the most frequent spelling of the name. Dunblane means the dun or fort of Blane and from that derivation an explanation of St Blane's involvement with Dunblane has been put forward. It has been suggested that St. Blane set up a fort on Holmhill where he also established a monastery. The flat plateau below Holmhill overlooking the river where the Cathedral now stands was identified as a possible place of worship for the lay people of the region. The discovery of a Pictish standing stone embedded in the walls of the Chapter House when the Cathedral was being restored in the late 19th century gave some credence to this theory about the possible siting of the place where the laity worshipped. Unfortunately a problem with the above explanation is that it was very unusual, but not unheard of, for monasteries in the 6th or 7th century to be placed inside forts.

An additional problem is that the place-name "Dunblane" has according to Dr Hutchison Cockburn 28 different spellings. Worse from the traditional point of view the late Marjorie Anderson of St Andrews University in 1955 favoured an early alternative spelling of the settlement we know as Dunblane. She found the word "Dul Blaan" being used in the 10th century Pictish Chronicle. The word "Dul" means a meadow so "Dul Blaan", translates as Blaan's meadow. Marjorie Anderson points out that the word "Dul" was frequently used in Scottish place names and was quite often followed by the name of a saint. If this alternative interpretation is accepted it is unlikely that there ever was a fort at Dunblane and the place-name "Dul Blaan" offers no guidance on the location or indeed the existence of a monastery

One important point however that can be made as a result of this discussion is that there is clear agreement that the town of Dunblane or "Dul Blaan" was closely associated with the 7th century British St Blane or Blààn giving the town a very early origin. Further whether St Blane's relics were moved from Kingarth to Dunblane at the time of the Viking invasions as Alex Woolf suggests is less important than the fact that they were transferred at some point before the Middle Ages. Their movement across for then a long distance and from Dal Riata to Central Scotland implies a very strong connection of a religious nature between St Blane and Dunblane though it is likely that its exact form will never be known to us.

Christianity in Scotland 600 - 1000 AD

It is likely that from 600 AD the Celtic Church, building mainly on St Columba's reputation and operating from settlements like Iona, gradually increased its influence in Scotland especially north of the Forth. At the same time the Catholic Church was gaining growing influence following Pope Gregory the Great's decision to send St Augustine on a mission to Britain in 596. Like St Ninian and St Columba, St Augustine was sent to consolidate Christianity in a country where it was already widespread. Inevitably tensions arose between the leaders of the Celtic and Catholic churches. The principal difference between the two churches was the date of Easter which was settled in favour of the Catholic Church at the Synod of Whitby chaired by King Oswy of Northumbria in 664.

Much has been made of the differences between the Celtic and Catholic churches, one being seen as mainly monastic and the other episcopal with the Catholic Church coming out victorious. The Celtic Church has been portrayed as the inspired converters of Dark Age Europe especially of Scotland, England and Germany through their monastic system. In contrast the Roman Church has been viewed as the successful organiser consolidating the gains of the Celtic missionaries with its system of bishoprics.

Recently this view has been abandoned by historians in the face of convincing evidence. It has been shown by studies of the Celtic and Roman churches that both the churches placed a lot of emphasis on monasteries and on bishops. So in the Roman Church one of their main driving forces was the creation of new monastic orders, many of the abbots doubling as bishops. Equally the Celtic Church placed considerable emphasis on bishops. Thus when Pictland was dominated by the Celtic Church from the 8th to 11th centuries a comprehensive network of bishoprics was set up with chief and subordinate bishops. Increasingly the two churches are being seen as very similar with the Celtic Church being viewed as a local version of Catholicism with Celtic practices, gradually giving way to Roman usage.

Since Dunblane was in Pictland it is important to establish what we know of the church in this part of Scotland between 700 and 1000 AD. Christianity was present in Pictland as early as the 5th century. It seems that its hold strengthened in the 7th century with the Celtic Church becoming increasingly significant. The Pictish Kings, with the possible exception of Nechtan in the early eighth century, furthered the hold of the Church establishing monasteries and organising the country into sees culminating in King Onuist's (c729-761) foundation of the See of St Andrews. It is possible that the increasing influence of the Celtic Church became total dominance under Kenneth MacAlpine who in 849 made Dunkeld the chief church in Southern Pictland and brought St Columba's relics to Dunkeld making that church the shrine of the saint. The hold of the Celtic Church can be demonstrated by the eventual dominance of Gaelic in Pictland as opposed to the indigenous Pictish language. Of course the kings benefited from this relationship because in return for royal patronage the church gave the kings unconditional support.

Part of the front panel of the St Andrews sarcophagus possibly showing King David as a hunter. The sarcophagus is a superb piece of Pictish art which may have been intended to hold the remains of the King Onuist.

(RCAHMS. Licensor www.scran.ac.uk)

It is also possible to reconstruct how the church operated at a local level. Texts of the period describe how a kingdom was divided into tuaths or tribal areas ruled by local leaders. Each tuath through their leaders entered into a relationship with the church. In return for the services of a priest the tuath provided tithes to support the priests. At the same time it is likely that the tuaths built small churches initially at least of wood to serve local communities. Each tuath had a chief bishop to control the clergy and maintain the church within its boundaries.

This may be an oversimplified description of how bishoprics emerged in Scotland north of the Forth. The picture was complicated by the foundation of monasteries which were powerful independent agents in the spread of Christianity. The monasteries will have led to the splintering of a tuath and of course from the monasteries bishops frequently emerged. It is also likely that over time the tuaths or tribal areas may have lost their coherence.

Was Dunblane the centre of a tuath with a chief bishop at its head? We probably will never know for certain. All we know definitely is that Dunblane had a bishop in 1160 called Lawrence who is referred to in documents of the period. The issue which historians have debated is whether the Bishopric of Dunblane was founded in the mid 12th century presumably by the reforming David 1 or was a much older foundation.

When was the Bishopric of Dunblane founded?

Geoffrey Barrow, the distinguished mediaevalist, gave some attention to this issue in his book *Kingship and Unity 1000 - 1306* which is still very much current even though it was first published some thirty years ago. In it he discusses how seven bishoprics were founded including Dunblane. He argues that their foundation must precede the mid 12th century because each of them has *"a profusion of detached portions (of land) often remote from the mother church."* He suggests that no 12th century king would have created bishoprics with such geographically illogical landholdings.

Geoffrey Barrow's arguments have considerable strength in the case of Dunblane (see the map below). In terms of geographical logic it is decidedly odd that its parishes extend some 30 miles to the north of the see but only five miles to the south. Important places north and south of the Forth and within ten miles of Dunblane are excluded for example Stirling, Alloa, St Ninians and Clackmannan. Yet Culross which is beyond these settlements is included. Also it is decidedly odd that St Madoes cut off by the river Tay from the rest of the diocese should be included within Dunblane and to the south that the diocese should have incorporated part of Kippen on the far side of the Forth. If Dunblane has any heartland as a Bishopric it appears to follow the frontier established by the Romans in the first century AD. In the north it starts at Abernethy goes along the Gask Ridge, down into Dunblane and includes parishes like Callander and Comrie which are adjacent to the hills leading into the Highlands where the Romans had some of their glen blocking forts.

If like Geoffrey Barrow you also consider the siting of Dunblane as a bishopric from the perspective of a 12th century monarch like David 1 it is odd. A better position for a bishopric in Central Scotland would surely have been Stirling, which was made a royal burgh by David and which has such a commanding position on the river Forth.

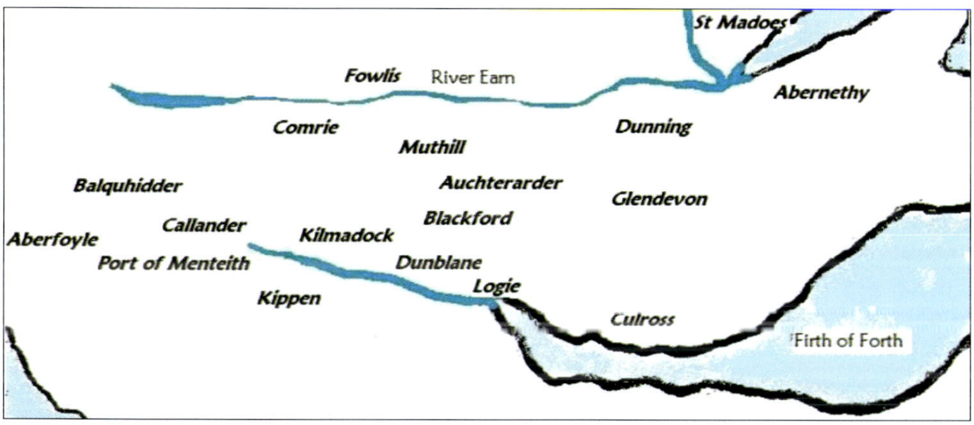

Map of the See of Dunblane in the Middle Ages showing its "detached portions of land" as described by Geoffrey Barrow.

Geoffrey Barrow's argument is supported by Richard Oram in his recent book *David 1 the King who made Scotland*. He states:

"No serious historian today would accept the assertion of mediaeval chroniclers that David found only three or four dioceses when he succeeded to the throne but left nine at the time of his death. There were several dioceses of clearly ancient origin but whether or not they had any incumbents on a regular basis throughout the 11th century is entirely a different matter." In other words Richard Oram considers that bishoprics like Dunblane were clearly ancient but were not always fully operative.

After describing the tidying up of the boundaries of the Bishopric of

Glasgow to give it coherence Richard Oram continues his analysis of King David's policy "As King after 1124, however, he made no attempt to do likewise with the existing Scottish bishoprics, as can be seen by the untidy fragmentation of their dioceses, which reflected the ancient distribution and acquisition of estates by the monasteries and early sees from which most evolved."

A third historian, Cynthia Neville, in her *Native Lordship in Mediaeval Scotland, The Earldoms of Strathearn and Lennox* in which she pays particular attention to the early history of the Bishopric of Dunblane has reiterated the view that the Bishopric was established well before the 12th century.

If a Bishopric was founded at Dunblane by the Picts when would it have been established? The 9th century is a distinct possibility. In that period the Picts were under intense pressure from the Vikings who had completely destroyed the monastic settlements on the islands of Scotland including Iona and Kingarth. Also there is Alex Woolf's intriguing suggestion that the relics of St Blane were transferred from the Isle of Bute during this period which might have coincided with the founding of a Bishopric at Dunblane to reinforce the Church in Central Scotland north of the Forth.

It is of course very frustrating not to be able to reach a firm conclusion on the date of the foundation of the Bishopric at Dunblane but one of the unfortunate consequences of being repeatedly invaded by the Vikings as the Picts were is the destruction of virtually all records.

Social and economic conditions in Scotland and Dunblane 410 - 1000 AD

Social and economic life in Scotland during the Dark Ages was dominated by the rulers and aristocratic elites in different parts of the country. There appear to have been a number of significant royal centres, north of the Forth, Dunadd in Dal Riata, Fortrui, Burghhead, Dundurn and Forteviot in Pictland, and Dumbarton, capital of the kingdom of Alt Clut or of Strathclyde. Forteviot which is close to Perth is likely to have been the site from which Pictland south of the Tay including Dunblane was dominated . To judge by excavations which have taken place at Dunadd, Dundurn and Dumbarton the kings and their companions had a high standard of life. All three forts traded extensively in a wide range of luxury goods with Europe and were centres of sophisticated metalwork.

Detail of the Dupplin Cross at Forteviot. There was probably a royal palace at Forteviot of which there is no trace today.
(photograph by Colin Storrar)

Despite this high quality of life these kings like rulers everywhere in the Dark Ages and much later were on the move for much of the year. They divided their realms into shires each with a royal residence, the caput in Pictland, where the ruler stayed for a significant time each year. During his stay in a shire the king and his household were supported by tribute in kind, that is food for example oats and barley and raw materials like wool and hides provided by the local landowners. The landowners in turn were supported by rent paid by their tenants in kind. It is interesting that even in the mid 17th century in Dunblane about 90% of rent was paid in kind – generally oats and barley, geese, hens, occasionally a sheep and frequently the performance of services such as providing the landowner with a number of cartloads of peat annually.

In addition to the tribute owed to the king and the rent due from the tenants, military service was also required from one level to another in the social hierarchy This was the only way in which kings and local rulers could raise armies in emergencies. It is known that Dark Age kings in Scotland had a number of young warriors at their courts who in return for food, the opportunity of military distinction and the grant of land formed the small inner core of the royal army. But these warriors were never more than a small force which had to be supplemented by the landowners and their dependants. By a miracle of survival a document from the 7th century Senchus Fer nAlban from Argyll has survived. A number of taxable households were listed within each kindred group. From them the number of men available for service was determined, in this case for rowing of boats in the navy. It is interesting that the taxable households were grouped into units of five possibly to reflect townships or small estates.

It is likely that the system of tribute and military service operated by the local rulers, landowners and their dependants was similar in Dunblane except of course that any military obligation was to serve in the army not the navy. Beyond that we have little secure knowledge about how farming, the main activity in a settlement like Dunblane in the Dark Ages was conducted, or what standard of life was enjoyed by the inhabitants.

The absence of firm knowledge about farming in Scotland in the Dark Ages and indeed into the mediaeval period is one of the scandals of modern archaeology. So much attention has been given to excavating Bronze and Iron Age settlements in Scotland and in forensic detail to the activities of the Romans, who were merely birds of passage in Scotland, and so little to agriculture, the main activity of the people over hundreds of years. It is only in the last few years that an attempt has been made to redress this imbalance by the establishment of a five year nation-wide project entitled Scotland's Rural Past (SRP) by the Royal Commission of Ancient and Historical Monuments Scotland (RCAHMS). SRP has the funding to support the training of local groups in the archaeological and research techniques which are needed to investigate abandoned agricultural sites. To date SRP has funded 62 local groups and some significant investigations are underway. Dunblane, like every parish in Scotland, has abandoned agricultural sites which may well date back to the Dark Ages and could well benefit from funding by SRP or its successor.

CHAPTER 6

SCOTLAND AND DUNBLANE IN THE EARLY MIDDLE AGES 1000 - 1286

Scotland 1000-1286 with special reference to King David 1 (1124-53)
During the years 1000-1286 we begin for the first time to encounter substantial documentary and architectural as opposed to archaeological evidence of the history of Dunblane. From 1160 we know the names of the bishops and some of their activities and of course we have the Cathedral Tower the first four storeys of which were built during this period.

It was a period that was important for Scotland and Dunblane. During these years the Kings of Alba originally the Kings of the Picts became virtually the Kings of Scotland. In 1018 Malcolm II with his ally King Owain of Strathclyde won the battle of Carham and in the resulting treaty gained undisputed control of the agriculturally rich and English speaking Lothian. Later in the century by a process that is still mysterious the Kingdom of Strathclyde was absorbed into Malcolm's kingdom or one of his successors. Thus by 1070 Malcolm III controlled what had been the Pictish heartland and all Lowland Scotland except for Galloway. In the next century David 1 (1124-53) overthrew the Kings of Moray who until then had been independent and established his hold on that area and its immediate hinterland. His successors William the Lion and Alexander II consolidated their grip on the kingdom especially in the south west and in the Highlands of Scotland. Finally in 1263 Alexander III won the battle of Largs against the Norwegians which ensured Scottish control of the Hebrides and the Isle of Man but not yet of Orkney or Shetland. So during this time the people of Dunblane were in the centre of what was becoming the Kingdom of Scotland.

At the same time the Kingdom underwent drastic change especially during the reign of King David 1. He was the son of Malcolm III and Queen Margaret. On account of the seizure of the throne by Malcolm's sons by his first marriage David spent much of his adolescence and young adulthood at the English court latterly acting as one of the chief advisers of Henry 1 of England (1100-35).

As a result when he became King of Scotland in 1124 he was very much an Anglo-Norman King ruling a Gaelic realm which he wanted to modernise. Change under him was wholesale earning him recently the title of *The King who made Scotland* by his most recent biographer Richard Oram. He set up a European system of justice through justiciars and sheriffs. He created a number of Royal Burghs one of which was Stirling. The inhabitants of a Royal Burgh were free of all taxation by local landlords and had a monopoly of overseas trade. David encouraged immigrants from England and the Low Countries with a wide range of skills to enrich the economy. For the first time money was minted in Scotland. But of most importance from the point of view of Dunblane he brought about wholesale changes in the church. A number of continental monastic orders were established in Scotland during David's reign, for example the Augustinians at Holyrood and at Cambuskenneth, the Cistercians at Melrose and at Kinloss in Moray and the Tironesians, first at Selkirk and then Kelso. At the same time the Bishoprics of St Andrews, and especially Glasgow, were strengthened with the dioceses north of the Forth including Dunblane being invigorated by the King.

Melrose Abbey the first Cistercian Abbey founded by King David 1 in 1136. The buildings on view are all from the 14th and 15th century, the earlier ones being destroyed by the armies of King Edward II in1322 and King Richard II in 1385.
(Charles McKean. Licensor www.scran.ac.uk)

The Bishopric of Dunblane before the arrival of Bishop Clement

The first surviving records of the Bishopric of Dunblane 1160 - 1233
Already the evidence for the Bishopric being established before the reign of King David 1 has been considered though the approximate date of its foundation is still only a matter of speculation. We are on more certain ground from the middle of the 12th century when the first bishop to be named in the records, Lawrence, witnesses a charter in 1160. From that date until the arrival of Clement in 1233 we can only establish a sketchy account of the bishops and some of their clergy drawing mainly on their witnessing of charters

There are two very useful descriptions of this period in the history of the bishopric; James Hutchison Cockburn's *Mediaeval Bishops of Dunblane* and Cynthia Neville's very recent book analysing the relationship between the early bishops of Dunblane and their chief patron the Earl of Strathearn in *Native Lordship in Mediaeval Scotland The Earldoms of Strathearn and Lennox.* Seven bishops are recorded for this period Lawrence c1160-1178, Symon 1178-1196, William 1196-1197, Jonathan 1198-1210, Abraham c1212- c1225, Ralph c1225-1226 and Osbert c1227-1230.

In addition at various times there appears to have been the following clergy serving in the diocese who are listed below with their responsibilities:

a Chancellor (administering the bishops court)
an Archdeacon (disciplining the clergy of the diocese),
a Dean (running groups of parishes),
a Treasurer (in charge of the income of the diocese)
a Rex Scholarum de Dunblane (responsible for the scholars in Dunblane)
a Rex Scholarum de Muthil (responsible for the scholars in Muthill)
and a small number of Bishop's Chaplains

The ecclesiastical seal of Bishop Symon 1178-1196.
(by kind permission of Dunblane Museum photograph by Len Bovill)

Despite these appointments Hutchison Cockburn and Neville are agreed that the whole staff needed to run a diocese were never in existence at any one time and as a result there would not have been a properly functioning Chapter during this period. The Bishop would be advised at this time in Neville's words by a "motley group of clerics".

It is also clear that during this period and indeed subsequently the Earl of Strathearn as chief patron of the diocese of Dunblane had a great deal of power over the development of the bishopric. His estate and that of the diocese were virtually coterminous with the result that no other landowner could challenge the Earl's control of the diocese. This dominance was recognised locally in the 12th and 13th centuries with the bishops and dignatories of the Cathedral being described as of Strathearn as opposed to of Dunblane. Externally the Earl's status in the diocese was recognised by the Pope who addressed him as the Chief Patron of the diocese and informed him of all the major decisions made by the Papal See in the diocese. It is also accepted by historians that especially before the appointment of Clement the bishops of Dunblane may have been selected by the Earl from the clerics in his own household though that can only be confirmed with certainty in the case of Bishop Abraham c1212-c1225.

As a result of Cynthia Neville's research we also have quite detailed knowledge of the activities of the Earl in the first twenty years of the 13th century in particular in his relationship with the Abbey of Inchaffray. At this time the Abbey was being transformed from a Celi Dei or Culdee monastery of considerable age into an Augustinian monastery. The Celi Dei monks were drawn from the long standing traditions of the Celtic Church which was very influential in Scotland. For these monks the highest religious state was that of the hermit in mystical contemplation of God.

Sadly virtually nothing is left today of the Abbey of Inchaffray. Perhaps the most impressive survival has been that of a papal seal discovered near the abbey. It is the seal of Pope Honorius III (1216-1227) and will have been attached to a letter or document sent to the abbey by the Pope.

(National Museums Scotland. Licensor www.scran.ac.uk)

In this respect their beliefs were similar to the monasteries of the early Eastern Mediterranean churches as opposed to the Roman Catholic monasteries with their emphasis on a communal religious life. From 1200 the Earl introduced Augustinian monks at Inchaffray though the Celi Dei monks were apparently undisturbed and he had buildings constructed to house the new monks. This expensive change was funded by the Earl diverting generous grants of income from the churches of Strageath, Auchterarder, Kinkell, Fowlis, Gask, Dunning and Monzievaird as well as menial income (that is food) from the church lands of Muthill, Abernethy and Tulliallan all of which could have gone to the diocese of Dunblane. The Earl also made some direct grants of land as well as of food from his own kitchen. Though during this period the Earl did make grants to the Bishopric of Dunblane he clearly favoured Inchaffray over the see and this preference was to threaten the very existence of the Bishopric of Dunblane when Clement became Bishop.

The Cathedral Tower at Dunblane

Also from this period are the first four courses of the Cathedral Tower: one of the oldest buildings in Scotland. Early buildings that have survived in Scotland that is built before 1200, fall into two groups. The first are of Irish (Celtic) design probably from the 9th and 10th centuries for example the Round Towers at Brechin and at Abernethy. The second group of buildings including the Cathedral Tower at Dunblane date from the 11th and 12th centuries and are Romanesque in style, that is imitating the Roman style of building often very crudely, with round arches for their doors, arcades and windows.

The Cathedral Tower at Dunblane repays some study starting with the outside of the building. First of all only the first four courses of the tower were built in the 11th or 12th centuries, the top two, the battlements and the spire were added in the fifteenth century. You will notice immediately that the stonework of the walls of the early part of the tower is much darker and cruder than the rest of the Cathedral which was constructed in the

The Cathedral Tower at Dunblane.

thirteenth century. It is likely that the stone of the tower came from a local source, transport of heavy material like stone being very difficult at the time. Then you will observe the distinctive windows which only appear on the fourth storey of the building, possibly for defensive reasons. The windows lower down are of an indeterminate age.

There are three of these windows visible on the east, south and west walls of the tower and they are round not pointed. This places them in the Romanesque period which ended about 1180 with the introduction of the pointed arch. This is a highly significant change since the weight bearing capacity of a pointed arch is much greater than that of a rounded arch. This development allowed mediaeval church builders to erect much taller buildings with much more slender and elegant arches than previously. If you study the window carefully you will see that another of its features is that it is recessed with the actual glass at the back of the arch and not either side of the pillar. It is likely that there was no glass in the original window. Identical windows and other marked similarities are evident in two other church towers locally, St Serfs at Dunning and the early church tower at Muthil. It looks as if the same craftsmen built both towers.

A close up of the windows on the fourth storey of the Cathedral Tower.

Church Tower at St Serfs Dunning with windows identical to those at Dunblane.
(photograph by Colin Storrar)

There is one further comparison that is worth making with regard to the windows at Dunblane and Dunning. They appear to be similar to the windows at a number of English churches, for example in the towers of St Michael's at the North Gate, Oxford (see next page) and Earls Barton in Northamptonshire to identify only two examples. These English examples are all considered to have been built in the late Saxon period, that is in the first half of the 11th century. This dating clashes with the generally accepted period for the building of the tower in Dunblane which Richard Fawcett places in the middle 12th century. It is of course possible that there was a stylistic lag between Scotland and England.

If you go inside the Cathedral you will be able to enter the Tower. You will notice the entrance to the Tower has a round arch and surprisingly no decoration in the tympanum that is the space between the lintel and the arch. The room at the bottom of the tower has a large recess in the middle of the east wall beneath a large round arch that looks as if it might have

Church windows at St Michael's at the North Gate in Oxford 1000-1050 - similar if rather more crude than the windows in the Tower of Dunblane Cathedral.
(by kind permission of the Vicar of St Michael's)

been an altar. The holes in the roof of this room show that at some time the room has been used for bell ringing. One puzzle is that the roof of this room is supported by pointed arches which is not consistent with the overall style of the building unless the original roof has been replaced at some later time. The rooms above are worth visiting if only to see the ringing chamber and the bells. The view from the parapet over Dunblane is breathtaking.

Bishop Clement 1233 - 1258

The significance of Clement's appointment as Bishop of Dunblane

Just when the Bishopric of Dunblane appeared to be in serious decline, with its chief patron the Earl of Strathearn favouring the Abbey of Inchaffray the see had a dramatic change of fortune. A new energetic priest, Clement, leader of the first group of Dominican friars to come to Scotland was appointed Bishop of Dunblane in 1233. He was not chosen by the local magnate, the Earl of Strathearn, whose family had dominated his predecessors but by a committee set up by Papal Mandate of three Scottish bishops, St Andrews, Brechin and Dunkeld thereby guaranteeing him unprecedented freedom of action which he was to use to good effect.

Clement's appointment was not an isolated event. It happened during a period in which the Church in Western Europe was very strong and it is necessary to digress briefly to examine why the Church experienced such success at this time because it will throw light on Clement and his career as Bishop of Dunblane.

In the second half of the 12th century the Papacy was under intense pressure. Especially in France and Italy there was widespread and trenchant criticism of the way in which the Church had abandoned the religious life based on poverty which had been such a central part of Christ's ministry. Instead the Popes, Archbishops, Bishops and even the monasteries had become wealthy and worldly. The crisis was so serious that there was a danger of new sects or churches being formed hostile to the Papacy as was to happen 350 years later at the time of the Reformation.

The emergence of the friars in the early 13th century of whom the main orders were the Franciscans and the Dominicans was itself related to the need for the Church to be reformed. Central to the philosophy of St Francis and St Dominic was a religious life based on poverty. Initially it was touch-and-go whether the Papacy would accept these new orders which appeared to challenge the Church's way of life, but the Popes quickly realised that if integrated into the Church they could provide the perfect answer to the critics. Almost immediately the friars were at the head of the Papal campaign to suppress the opposition. For example St Dominic who founded the Black Friars of which Clement was a member led the mission to reclaim the heretical Albigensians in Southern France.

The success of this campaign against heresy strengthened the position of the Papacy enabling the Popes to expand the policy to include the imposition of orthodoxy throughout the area controlled by the Church. At the same time the position of the Church in relation to kings was enhanced giving the Church more independence from lay influence. Hand in hand with this resurgence the Popes encouraged the building and rebuilding of Cathedrals.

Clement's career in Scotland should be considered in relation to this resurgence of the Church in the first half of the 13th century. The first mission of Black Friars to arrive in Scotland led by Clement was clearly of great importance in reinforcing the power of the Church. They reached Scotland in 1228 only 12 years after their order had been founded. As such they were first generation of Black Friars and it is usually the case that the first generation of any church or religious order is the most determined and pure in their beliefs. Clement himself about whose early life we know nothing except that he was a Scot entered the Order in Paris in 1219 only three years after it was founded so that it is likely that he was an intimate of St Dominic himself. It is clear that he was something of a star.

Clement's mission as a Black Friar was very successful. Eight friaries were set up in the poorest parts of Scottish towns, one of them in Stirling hence Friars Street. All the houses were very popular with the people whom they served. The Black Friars were especially noted for their rigorous approach to their life of poverty. Unlike the Franciscans who confined their vows of poverty to the friars themselves but allowed the friaries to own property and money the Dominicans extended their vow of poverty to the friaries as well. Within five years of his arrival in Scotland Clement was appointed Bishop of Dunblane by Papal Commission, the first Black Friar to be appointed a Bishop in Britain. Ten years later he was asked by the King to act in addition as Bishop of Argyll. This was a dangerous and difficult assignment since the King had virtually no control over the province. So Clement was in the rare position of holding two sees at once, one of them being unusually challenging.

The state of the Cathedral and Diocese as reported by Clement on his arrival in Dunblane

Our knowledge of the state of the Cathedral and Bishopric of Dunblane on Clement's arrival in 1233 is entirely dependent on his own description, our only source. As such it has to be treated with some caution because it is the account which he gave to the Papal Commission in Rome which considered the state of the diocese. Clement had gone to the Papal Court to persuade the Pope to make changes in the management and funding of the diocese and as a result he may have exaggerated the poor state of the Cathedral and

Bishopric. However it is worth spending some time on Clement's account because it is our first description of life in Dunblane.

Clement states that when he arrived in Dunblane he found that the church was "roofless". It is interesting that his description confirms that the Cathedral had a predecessor and that Clement called it a "church", possibly the term Cathedral was not yet in general use. It is likely that the church found by Clement was attached to or alongside the tower that still exists. He found only one priest officiating there. For a church that was the centre of a diocese this was an appalling state of affairs. Such a church should have had at least six services each day with up to 20 clergy officiating. Worse, he describes the priest as a "rural chaplain". The word "rural" is probably significant implying that the priest was of a low standard only fit for a rural parish as opposed to a church that was the centre of a diocese. It may even have implied that the priest was illiterate.

The Choir of Glasgow Cathedral built in the first half of the 13th century which Clement will have been aware of and contrasted with conditions on his arrival at Dunblane in 1233.

(University of Strathclyde. Licensor www.scran.ac.uk)

Even more important Clement states that the diocese had no Chapter. The Chapter was the body or committee of clergy who ran the business of a diocese and was responsible for maintaining the daily round of services. The Chapter included the Dean who acted for the Bishop in his absence, the Archdeacon who was responsible for the discipline of the clergy in the diocese, the Treasurer who guarded the finances of the Bishopric, the Chancellor its legal officer as well as the ordinary canons many of whom would hold benefices in the bishopric. This deplorable state of affairs Clement attributed to the woeful lack of income at Dunblane, the bishops allowing it to be siphoned off by the local landowners. Clement brings his description to life by stating that what revenues were left would scarcely sustain him for six months and that he had 'nowhere to lay his head', that is there was no bishop's palace or lodging in Dunblane or anywhere in the diocese.

Although Clement's account of the state of the diocese and of the Cathedral has to be treated with some caution since he was pleading his case before the Pope, in many respects it appears to have been accurate if somewhat exaggerated. As the diocese did not have a functioning Chapter it did not have the basic system of management which was considered essential for running an efficient diocese in the Middle Ages. Also the revenues of the diocese had been squeezed over the years by local land-owners. However it is interesting that Clement does not mention any landowners by name least of all the Earl of Strathearn whom he presumably did not wish to offend. The Earl had indeed seized a lot of the income of the churches in the diocese which might have been expected to go to the bishop but he had diverted it to a religious cause in the endowment of the Abbey of Inchaffray. In so doing the Earl was behaving in the same way as other important landowners in Scotland. As Cynthia Neville points out they preferred to support abbeys because they could control them more effectively than bishoprics: with their wide responsibilities bishoprics were much more independent than abbeys. It is not possible to verify the poor state of the Cathedral and the state of the religious services being conducted within its walls but what Clement describes is consistent with a diocese that had no Chapter, was starved of funds and whose last bishop before Clement, Osbert, appears to have retired to Holyrood Abbey rather than face the rigours of being the bishop of Dunblane.

Effigy of a Knight and his Lady in the middle of the north aisle of Dunblane Cathedral which may be of one of the mediaeval Earls of Strathearn with his Countess
(photograph by Len Bovill)

Clement's campaign to invigorate the Bishopric

Clement's first action to establish the bishopric on firmer foundations was to go to Rome and put his case before the Pope. The Pope appears to have given Clement his full support. Presumably to speed up the decision making he remitted the case to a committee of three Scottish bishops, St Andrews, Brechin and Dunkeld, the same committee who had appointed Clement in the first place. The Pope took the precaution of outlining a settlement suggesting that a quarter of the teinds in each parish in the diocese should be given to the see. Teinds, more usually called tithes, were an annual tax amounting to 10% of the agricultural produce of the parish levied to support the clergy. The Pope also suggested that additional income for the diocese should be found from churches owned by the powerful abbeys of Cambuskenneth and Arbroath. With this money Clement was to erect a residence for the bishop and appoint a Dean and Chapter to run the diocese. Finally as a fallback position should his plan prove unacceptable the Pope proposed that control of the bishopric should reside with the Abbey of Inchaffray - what Clement's position would have been if that had happened was not made clear.

The settlement proposed by the Pope not surprisingly was accepted by the three bishops but Clement found it difficult to implement. He spent years negotiating with landowners and local abbeys for an increased income but usually had to compromise because much of the money had been allocated already to local religious houses such as the Abbey of Inchaffray by the Earl of Strathearn. A typical encounter was between the Clement and the Earl of Menteith. The Earl appealed against the decision taken by the bishops and refused to hand over the teinds due in the parishes on his estate because he wanted to found a House of Augustinian Canons on the island of Inchmaholm and for this he needed funds. Eventually after a lengthy dispute a compromise was reached. Clement agreed that he would surrender all claim to an income from the lands of the Earl of Menteith except for the parishes of Kippen and Callander and the Earl was free to found his priory which he did.

Remains of the Priory Church at Inchmaholm. The Priory was founded by Walter Comyn, Earl of Menteith in 1237. He was the Earl of Menteith who was in dispute with Bishop Clement over the teinds of parishes on his estate which the Earl wanted to use for endowing the Priory.

(photograph by Colin Storrar)

As a result Clement's campaign to establish Dunblane as a strong independent see was of limited effect. Even some years after his death his successors were only exercising full control over just under half of the 26 parishes in the diocese and even then in some cases were only receiving cash payments as opposed to teinds. Cash payments were much inferior to teinds because they were vulnerable to inflation - teinds being paid in kind were immune to inflation. Due to this lack of money Clement found it difficult to fund enough canons and prebends to establish a viable Chapter. Indeed Cynthia Neville asserts that it was only in 1270 twelve years after Clement's death that the Chapter was finally stabilised.

Despite this lack of success financially Clement's episcopacy in Dunblane was an extraordinary success because he made the bold and far sighted decision to rebuild the Cathedral on an unexpectedly grand scale – a task which he and his successor Robert de Prebenda saw through to completion and which will now be described.

Rebuilding Dunblane Cathedral c 1240 - c 1285

Clement's decision to rebuild the Cathedral

Clement's decision to scrap the existing building and erect a new Cathedral was extraordinary even though it was in line with the then Papal policy. Building a Cathedral in the Middle Ages was a massive project analogous, given our much greater resources, to rebuilding the Forth Road Bridge today. It is also clear from the foundations of the building that from the outset Clement intended the Cathedral to be a very big building for its period in Scotland. Large quantities of stone had to be quarried, transported and prepared for construction. Workers of all sorts had to be recruited, especially stone masons, joiners, sculptors and artists, many from abroad. All the materials had to be purchased and the workers paid, fed and housed for years. Even more daunting, building a Cathedral took a long time to complete, up to 50 years, so Clement was starting a project that he knew only his successors could bring to fruition.

All this was being attempted in a diocese that was one of the poorest in Europe in a country that was also very poor compared with its neighbours. The resources available to Clement from the diocese were limited.

Even though only the chancel and aisles of Dornoch Cathedral survive it is clearly on a smaller scale than Dunblane Cathedral. It is however much more typical of the sort of building which could be afforded by dioceses in mediaeval Scotland outside the main cities.

(St Andrews University Library. Licensor www.scran.ac.uk)

Worse, Scotland had very little wealth to spare for a project like building a Cathedral. Agriculture which was the main economic activity of the country was dominated by subsistence farming except possibly in the wheat producing areas of Lothian, Angus and Fife. The summer was very short and the only crops that could be grown were oats with a small amount of barley. There was a growing market in wool for export but no sign of the textile industry that was making the Netherlands, France and parts of Italy so wealthy and was to have such an impact on Southern England in the 14th and 15th centuries. In addition Scotland was away from the main trade routes of the period and as a result its trade and manufacturing were undeveloped. Consequently there was little surplus wealth in the country to help a poor diocese like Dunblane in such a massive building project.

How then was the rebuilding of Dunblane Cathedral financed? We don't know. It is reasonable to assume that the income of the diocese which would largely be devoted to the project was supplemented by money from the Papacy. It is likely that such funds were intermittent and this will explain why it took so long to build with short spurts of activity and long intervals when no resources were available.

Three strategies for describing the building of the Cathedral
analysing style, focussing on construction and examining aims

If we are trying to describe the construction of a well known building erected in the last three or four centuries in Scotland we are often able to draw on records such as the plans of the architect, the accounts of the builders and even descriptions of different phases of the construction and the problems encountered. Unfortunately no such records exist in the case of Dunblane Cathedral. If such papers had survived until the Reformation they were probably destroyed either in the summer of 1559 under the direction of the leading Protestant Reformers or they may have been taken abroad in the mid 1560s by Bishop William Chisholm II and subsequently lost. Despite this absence of documents historians are still able to throw a lot of light on how this would be done.

The first consideration in describing the building of a cathedral church or abbey is *stylistic*. Professor Richard Fawcett uses this approach in his book *Scottish Cathedrals* which was published over ten years ago. He analyses minutely the style of building used in each phase of the construction of the Cathedral and compares it with similar styles elsewhere. Such a comparison enables him to date the different stages of the construction to within a decade and to embed the building within the architectural context of the time. This approach is particularly fruitful in the case of Dunblane because its rebuilding in the 13th century was part of the great Gothic movement originating in the Île de France about 1150 and sweeping through France, Germany and the British Isles before petering out about 1290. It is reckoned that during this period of Gothic building 80 cathedrals and 500 abbeys and churches were either built from scratch or substantially reconstructed. The Gothic movement was like a great surge of activity with Dunblane at its outer extremity. Professor Fawcett's account using the stylistic approach follows.

A view of Salisbury Cathedral, built slightly earlier than Dunblane Cathedral. Salisbury has always seemed to me to have the most beautiful exterior of all Gothic buildings in Britain, if not in Europe.

(Photograph by Steve Day, Visitor Services Salisbury Cathedral)

A second approach which is employed by historians describing the Gothic movement in general is to focus on how a cathedral church or abbey was *constructed* making use of documents where they survive and generalising from them to other buildings constructed at the time but where the relevant records have not survived. This approach focuses on construction rather than the style of the building. For example the same problems of construction had to be overcome and the same range of skilled and unskilled workers will have been employed in every Gothic Cathedral and church. It is fortunate then that in other countries especially France and England a rich variety of documents relating to the construction of Gothic buildings has survived. For example lists of workers, contracts of employment and reports of how long a particular phase took to complete and the problems encountered have been preserved.

A third approach to describing the building of Cathedrals is to focus on the *aims of the builders*. The aims of the builder can be deduced partly from the size, layout and decoration of Cathedrals, Dunblane Cathedral being a good example, if not on the grand scale, compared with Cathedrals in England and on the continent of Europe. Light on the purposes behind the building of Cathedrals and other large churches in the middle ages can also be shed by studying the writings of mediaeval clerics,

The style of building employed at Dunblane Cathedral

A short tour of Dunblane Cathedral at this point will help readers to appreciate the style of the building and the main phases of construction. For a more detailed and far more authoritative account readers should consult Richard Fawcett's *Scottish Cathedrals*, the main source of this brief description.

The best starting point for a tour of the Cathedral is from the garden in the north east corner of the graveyard. In front of you attached to the Chancel is a two storey rectangular building, the Chapter House, which was the first part of the Cathedral to be reconstructed. It was designed to accommodate on the ground floor a room where the Chapter met to make decisions concerning the management of the diocese and above the library and treasury of the diocese. The building may also have been where Clement lived when in Dunblane so that he did at least have somewhere to lay his head.

The Chapter House and northern face of Dunblane Cathedral.

How do we know that this rectangular building was the first part of the Cathedral to be reconstructed? We can make this statement with some confidence because of the style of the windows. They are all simple lancet windows that is they are shaped like a lance, albeit a rather fat one, with no additional decoration. If you now look at other parts of the north face of the Cathedral you will notice that some of the windows while having lancets also have additional decoration at the top and that others are very much larger and more elaborately decorated. These important differences allow us to date the other parts of the Cathedral as later than the Chapter House. You may consider the lancet windows to be rather plain but they were the only form of window used in the first hundred years of Gothic architecture from 1150 to 1250, and in Scotland from c1200 to c1250. Placed in a line they are rather elegant and they dominate buildings like Glasgow and Salisbury Cathedrals to excellent effect. Perhaps the most striking use of the lancet window is the Five Sisters in the north transept of York Minster. Since it is unlikely that the construction of the Chapter House started much before the early 1240s the building can probably be dated to that decade.

The Five Sisters at York Minster.

(by kind permission of the Dean and Chapter of York Minster)

Before moving on it is worth emphasising one other feature of the Chapter House, *viz.*

its shape. Many readers especially from south of the border will think of Chapter Houses as being round and much larger than the one at Dunblane. The geometry of Chapter Houses simply differed north and south of the border with most of the English Chapter Houses being round and nearly all Scottish being rectangular. The size also reflects the differing size of dioceses in England and Scotland.

The Nave of Dunblane Cathedral from the West Door.
(photograph by Len Bovill)

You should now move to the second vantage point from which to view the Cathedral – that is at the west end of the Nave. The route you can take is *via* the south porch and past the Cathedral Tower. Once you are at the west end of the Nave you are at the place from where the architects of the building wanted it to make most impact. In all cathedrals, and Dunblane is no exception, the West Door was used for the triumphal entry of processions to the Cathedral and the buildings were designed to enhance that experience.

As you stand at the west end of the Nave looking along the arcade you become aware of how your eyes are drawn deliberately towards the Altar and the most sacred part of the Cathedral. At the same time, and almost in competition, the pillars of the Arcade lead your eye upwards to the Clerestory. It is difficult to cater for taste but you will probably also be struck by the elegance of the Arcade supported by piers that are decorated by a number of shafts with their motifs being extended into the arch above. Even more impressive are the arches in the Clerestory which is just above the Arcade with two arches to every opening at ground level. It is very much a matter of taste but I prefer a Gothic Arcade and Clerestory with its line of pointed arches to the heavier pillars and rounded arches of the Romanesque style which immediately preceded the Gothic. Before leaving your vantage point at the west end of the Nave look behind you and you will see 6 carved canon's stalls from the late 15th or early 16th century which were originally in the Choir. They are elaborately carved and repay study.

If you look at the windows in the Clerestory carefully, especially those to the north, you will become aware of a change of style half way between the east and west end of the Nave. Initially the windows are all simple lancets as in the Chapter House. But then some decoration appears in the form of tracery at the top of the windows and between the arches in the Clerestory. The same theme is taken up in the much larger window at the west end of the Cathedral. These windows are later than the simple lancet windows of the Chapter House and are in the very first stage of what is called the

Decorated phase of Gothic architecture placing the completion of the nave at about 1270.

You should now move forward to the Chancel and for best effect stand just where the Choir Stalls begin on the same side as the organ. You will immediately become aware of a change of style – the windows are much larger than those in the Chapter House and in the Nave. The six windows to the south and the east window seem to take up nearly all the wall. Particularly impressive are the six windows on the south wall of the Chancel which give you a feeling of a triumphal processional way leading to the Altar. Unfortunately only the outer dimensions of these windows are original - the tracery which you see today is from the early 19th century. However the size of the windows relative to the wall space indicates that the Chancel is the last part of the Cathedral to be reconstructed probably being completed by the mid 1280s.

The Clerestory Windows showing the change of style half way down the Nave.

The Chancel was designed in the Middle Ages to be the most sacred part of the Cathedral. Often cut off from the Nave by a large screen known as the Rood Screen it was the place where members of the Chapter or their substitutes conducted at least seven services every day of the year. It is likely that their stalls were placed up against the north and south walls of the Chancel with the space in between being vacant. The glass that filled the windows in 1290 is of course long gone but the present glass which was installed in the early 20th century is of a high standard. It is most impressive at certain times in the day when the sun is at a particular angle and the Chancel is flooded with coloured light. Today the Chancel of Dunblane Cathedral with its large windows and impressive glass retains much of the mediaeval atmosphere. Again along the walls of the Choir close to the Altar you will see a number of late mediaeval choir stalls which are of a high artistic standard, four of which are highlighted on the cover of this book. As you leave the Cathedral it is worth going into the Chapter House which opens off the Chancel. It is the only part of the Cathedral to have stone vaulting and is attractive though obviously on a small scale.

The construction of Dunblane Cathedral

So far our account of the rebuilding of Dunblane Cathedral has been based on evidence drawn from the building today. Special emphasis for example has been put on the size of the windows in the different parts of the building which makes it possible to date the sequence of construction with reasonable certainty.

But there are a lot of questions left unanswered by this approach – in fact it raises more questions than it answers. So we are left wondering who were the people responsible for building the Cathedral? Who were the chief architects and planners of the building? Were the Bishops, especially Clement, involved in the choice of designs? What types of skilled and unskilled men worked on the Cathedral? Were they local or from abroad? What types of tools and machines were available to the builders? Where did the stone come from and how was it transported to Dunblane? Even though no documents survive from the building of Dunblane Cathedral, the uniformity of the Gothic movement across Western Europe allows us to describe what will almost certainly have happened at Dunblane from records that throw light on the building of cathedrals in England, France and Germany which do survive.

The architects and planners of Dunblane Cathedral

Every major building project needs planners and architects, and constructing a cathedral in the 13th century was a massive undertaking relative to the assets available. There are a significant number of cathedrals, abbeys and churches for which we have documentary evidence about the people who were in control of the project. Three individuals dominated the planning and management of these large undertakings.

First there was the *Significatio*. He, and it nearly always was a 'he', was the person who had commissioned the building, often a king, but in the case of Dunblane almost certainly Bishop Clement and his successor, Bishop Robert de Prebenda (1259-1284).

Second was a man called the *Magisterium*. He was a priest or a layman hired, often annually, by the Significatio and the Cathedral Chapter to manage the preparations and then the actual building. He purchased materials, signed all contracts including with skilled workers and supervised the work day by day. He was almost what we would call a Master of Works. Of course we have no idea who the various Magisteriums were in the case of Dunblane and there will have been many of them during the 40-50 years when the Cathedral was being constructed.

Third there was the *Master Mason* or head of the masons. He was responsible for the overall design of the building and for dealing with major problems encountered during its construction, the closest modern equivalent being the chief architect of a building. One of the best known cases of a Master Mason was William of Sens, a Frenchman, who was commissioned to rebuild the Chancel of Canterbury Cathedral when it burnt down in 1174. He was selected only after a hunt on an international scale for the right man for the job. Again we don't know the names of any of the Master Masons who worked at Dunblane.

How did these three individuals, the Significatio, the Magisterium and the Master Mason interact and who was the most important for the design and control of the project? The Magisterium can be quickly excluded. He was a facilitator not a designer or planner. It was his task to see the work was carried out efficiently but he made no contribution to the overall design of the building, that was between the Significatio and the Master Mason.

We do know of Significatios who had enormous influence on the building of a church or a cathedral. For example King Henry III of England (1216-1272) took a great interest in church building, too much in the view of many of his noblemen! He was so impressed by the recently completed Sainte-Chapelle in Paris that he said that he would like it placed on a cart and transported to London. And when he came to have Westminster Abbey rebuilt he insisted that it should be constructed according to the most recent French designs.

The rebuilt Chancel of Canterbury Cathedral designed by the Master Mason, William of Sens in the late 12th century.

(by kind permission of the Dean and Chapter of Canterbury Cathedral)

But Henry III was exceptional. Most Significatios were not as knowledgeable or interested in architecture as he was and generally had to spend long periods away from the construction site. For example, Bishop Clement, almost certainly the Significatio of Dunblane Cathedral, was away from the town for long periods. He served the King as Bishop of Argyll thus the Master Mason would have had a fairly free hand at Dunblane.

Identifying the Master Masons and their modus operandi

Who were these Master Masons who acted as chief architects of buildings like cathedrals? St Thomas Aquinas writing in the middle of the 13th century describes them as follows:

> *"Thus in building, the craftsman who designs the form of the building is called wise and architect as opposed to the subordinate craftsmen who hew wood and prepare stone."*

It is clear that the Master Masons were seen as top craftsmen not a professional group with separate qualifications like architects today. It is surprising to us that, in a period as stratified as the 13th century, the design of such vitally important buildings as cathedrals should be under the control of men of relatively humble origins. In France some of the best known Master Masons were able to build substantial houses for themselves and there is some evidence of sons following their fathers as Master Masons but as a group they were never of the same status as senior clergy or the lesser ranks of the landowning class.

Before leaving the planning of cathedrals there is one final query that needs to be raised and which puzzles many people. Did the Master Masons work to architectural plans in constructing these complex buildings over long periods of time? There is no evidence of architectural plans until the early 14th century by which time Dunblane Cathedral was complete. So amazingly it is likely that these humble Master Masons kept the designs of the whole building in their heads.

There are, however, drawings of parts of cathedrals such as the early 13th century sketches by Villard de Honnecourt of different features of French cathedrals under construction at the time. Also from about 1220 scratched drawings of individual parts of a cathedral have survived on walls and floors, which were probably used by workmen to guide them in constructing a window or a vault, so at least a part of a building followed a sketch plan. From the 13th century sixteen such drawings survive in France, twelve in England, nine in Germany and one in Dalmatia. None for this period have survived in Scotland but they were almost certainly used.

Scratched drawings on the walls of Rosslyn Chapel, near Edinburgh, which may be an outline of the building used by craftsmen during its construction in the 15th century.
(photograph by Simon Beattie)

The methods used to build a Cathedral like Dunblane in the 13th century

We can also piece together the process of building a cathedral, like Dunblane, from contemporary documents and illustrations.

The initial stage in the construction of any large building in the 13th century was a period of preparation before even a stone was laid. In the case of the Vale Royal Abbey in the south west of England in the mid 13th century the records show that the preparatory phase lasted three years with a range of tasks being completed.

The first task was the quarrying of stone and its transport to the site. Generally a local supply of stone was used because of the problems of transporting large and heavy loads. In the case of Dunblane Cathedral it is thought that the stone for the building came mainly from quarries at Bannockburn. Even though this was only a few miles away the transport of the stone will have been difficult. At the time there were very few carts and it is likely that sleds (sledges) were used. It is interesting that even as late as 1700 to judge from the inventories of deceased tenants in Dunblane carts were still very rare and highly prized and the main method of transporting goods was by sled or by packs slung over a horses back.

Once sufficient stone was gathered masons were recruited to prepare it for building. Already by the 13th century there was evidence of a degree of pre-fabrication in the construction of a building. The raw blocks of stone were cut into the correct sizes for different parts of the building. You can see at Dunblane Cathedral that all the stone used on the outer surface of the walls has been cut to provide a smooth exterior.

But stone was not the only preparation that was necessary before building could be begun. As is evident from the records of Vale Royal Abbey carpenters were employed to prepare planks for scaffolding and for roofing and the same will have occurred at Dunblane. Also smiths will have been required to hammer out the nails needed in the construction. The records at Vale Royal show that as many as many as 12,000 wooden boards and 67,000 iron nails were prepared in advance of building being begun.

The base course at Dunblane Cathedral which is the same all round the building.

(photograph by Len Bovill)

Finally as at Vale Royal Abbey there will have been a number of unskilled workers to prepare the living quarters for the skilled craftsmen; masons, roofers, carpenters, painters and even sculptors, who would come conceivably from as far as Europe as the building took shape. At the same time these labourers will have dug the foundations of the new Cathedral. It is interesting that in the case of Dunblane Cathedral Richard Fawcett writes as follows:

> *"on the evidence of the base courses the whole building was laid out in one operation."*

So the ground plan of the building will have been dug and laid out in stone as a first stage of construction.

Documentary evidence reveals that when construction actually began it was seasonal. Work on the construction stopped when the mortar froze which could be as early as mid-September though the 13th century was one of unusual warmth. Generally during the winter preparations continued for the next season with stones being carved for windows and with roof timbers being cut. Such arrangements would mean that any worker recruited from a distance might spend some years in Dunblane until his part in the building had been completed.

We also know from contemporary illustrations that quite sophisticated building techniques were in use even in the 13th century. It was a problem for the men constructing and decorating, for example painting, a large building in the Middle Ages to work at considerable heights. Apparently scaffolding was widely used. Alternatively vacant holes were often left in a wall as it rose and timbers were placed in the holes so that men could climb to whatever height was required. In some towers in Central Italy the gaps in the walls used during construction can still be seen.

It was also necessary during construction to raise heavy weights like large blocks of stone. By the 13th century when Dunblane Cathedral was being built simple machinery was being used to lift stone. Stones could be put in a basket, or held by a grab and hauled up by a rope over a cross-beam. Winches attached to a building were also common. Alternatively a simple crane was used which consisted of two upright posts joined with a length of rope round a crossbeam.

The aims of the Cathedral Builders illustrated by Dunblane Cathedral

So far we have focussed on two aspects of the rebuilding of Dunblane Cathedral - dating the different stages of building by examining its style and reconstructing the process of building through documentary sources. We have still however to consider the most important aspect of the rebuilding of the Cathedral, namely the aims of those responsible for the whole project. The best approach to this important theme is to consider the over-all purpose of building cathedrals at the time and their impact on the 13th century public, linking this to Dunblane.

The first striking feature of virtually all Gothic cathedrals, and Dunblane is no exception, is their size - in itself a statement of what the builders saw as the overwhelming power of God and of the power of the church. Even today as you travel down to London by train you are struck by York Minster visible miles away from the town and dwarfing even the modern buildings of the city. The area round Dunblane is far more undulating than the flat plains of Eastern England and Dunblane Cathedral is of course not as big as York Minster but the Cathedral still dominates the modern town of Dunblane and the farmland immediately around it. When it was first built its dominance will have been even more overpowering. In the 13th century very few houses in Dunblane were two storied and, even those that were, will have been very much smaller than two storied houses today. Out in the countryside the main type of house occupied by the population was like the Highland black house often so low that you could barely see them with their thatch roofs almost flush with the surrounding fields. Of course there were the castles of the king and the nobility but they were deliberately threatening and had forbidding and uninviting exteriors – cathedrals were welcoming and open to everyone.

The grim exterior of Dirleton Castle, largely built in the 13th century, and contemporary with the more welcoming Dunblane Cathedral.

(National Trust for Scotland. Licensor www.scran.ac.uk)

A second feature of Gothic Cathedrals, a cause of marvel to the mediaeval public and a further expression of the worship of God and of the power of the church is the huge uninterrupted well lit space of the interior of these buildings. The people of the Middle Ages were used to small dark interiors, even the castles of the King and nobility were divided into rooms with little light because of the need for defence. The Romanesque cathedrals and churches, which preceded the Gothic do have a beauty all their own but their interiors tend to be dark and mysterious not open and full of light like the Gothic. As the people of Dunblane stood, for example, at the West Door of the Cathedral they will have had an uninterrupted view to every corner of the building partially blocked only by the Rood Screen, which divided the Nave from the Chancel. Even the Rood Screen will not have entirely blocked the view of the Chancel with its large east window occupying most of the wall. It is interesting that it was not until the building of the Crystal Palace in the 1840s and the Victorian railway stations that such vast space was successfully recreated in buildings.

The interior of Glasgow Cathedral showing the Rood Screen which blocks our view of the Chancel and Altar except for an entrance in the middle of the screen. The Rood Screen would have been similar in Dunblane Cathedral.

(University of Strathclyde. Licensor www.scran.ac.uk)

We obviously don't know exactly how people reacted to the interior of Gothic cathedrals but we do know how the theologians who described the main purpose of a Gothic cathedral thought that they should react. For the theologians light was of supreme religious significance and was the most important element in the interior of a cathedral. Abbot Suger who more than anyone defined the purpose of Gothic cathedrals and churches saw light as enabling the ascent from the material to the spiritual through the aesthetic. For him the aesthetic quality was the dominating feature of their buildings. Writing in the middle of the 12th century he stated:

"Light is the determining element in the design of the church."

And again:

"The whole church appears in full glory the wonderful never ending light from the bright glowing glass permeating the beauty of the interior."

Bishop Grosseteste the leading English theologian, academic and churchman reinforced this view in the mid 13th century when the rebuilding of Dunblane Cathedral was in full swing. For him *"God is light"* – a phrase that is familiar to us.

And when applied to buildings like cathedrals he wrote:

"Physical light is the best, the most beautiful of all the bodies that exist. Light is what constitutes the perfection and beauty of bodily forms."

An example of the impact of coloured glass in the north east corner of the Nave of the Cathedral today.

(Photograph by Ewing Wallace)

So it is clear that through their size, internal space and above all light Gothic cathedrals were making a statement that would have been unmistakeable to 13th century people.

As well as filling people with awe of God and the Church the inside of Gothic Cathedrals were designed to instruct them. The builders of thirteenth century cathedrals introduced a new and, to the people of the period, perhaps a shocking depiction of Christ. Until then Christ had been presented in a formal and traditional manner with no attempt being made to depict his suffering and humanity. All this changed with the renovated and reconstructed cathedrals in the 13th century. Generally a wooden image of Christ on the cross was placed on top of the Rood Screen which divided the Chancel from the Nave from which it dominated the interior of the cathedral. Such portrayals were not only the first realistic depictions of Christ's suffering but it is generally accepted the first portrayals of suffering of any kind. Christ was shown as a human being in agony and then triumphantly as part of the Trinity giving ordinary human beings legitimate access to God through him. Such a presentation is likely to have been in the rebuilt Dunblane Cathedral. The depiction of Christ on the

Cross was of course always supported by other paintings of episodes in the bible story. Since most people were illiterate, and in any case the Bible was in Latin, and sermons were only preached occasionally, paintings were the chief means by which the population could gain an understanding of the Holy Word.

St Peter depicted on an altar piece c 1280 at Westminster Abbey just when Dunblane Cathedral was being completed.

(Copyright: Dean and Chapter of Westminster)

Concentrating, however, on one or two features of 13th century cathedrals perhaps falsifies the overall impression that the people will have gained of such buildings when they first came into use. Everywhere they looked, and the people of Dunblane will have had the same experience, there will have been something to catch the eye – not only the coloured light and the paintings but also the stonework all of which will have been painted to pick out the main architectural features of the building, the gold and jewels on the numerous altars in the aisles, the fur-lined vestments of the clergy glimpsed in processions and during services in the Chancel as well as the sumptuously decorated High Altar. Had we been there we would probably have been horrified by the almost cinematic presentation of the building so different from our cathedrals today with their cool reserved stonework. That all of this is not a fanciful impression of Dunblane Cathedral is shown by a petition from the clergy of Dunblane to the Pope in 1419 in which they informed His Holiness that their Cathedral:

"was of old most sumptuous in its building, its ornaments and vestments, its many relics and jewels."

Sight, however, was not the only sense to which these new and reconstructed buildings appealed. On entering them the people were assailed by a sound that is rare to visitors in any European cathedral today, that of services being conducted. Every day there was almost continual worship with up to nine services starting with Matins at 5.30am in the summer and 6.00am in the winter, and ending with Vespers and Compline in mid-evening. These services were conducted by the cathedral clergy. There were also services in the Nave for the local population and masses for the dead said in the aisles. The quality of the services, especially the nine performed daily in the Chancel, was high. A precentor was appointed responsible for the music and there was generally an organ on top of the Rood Screen. The services were also a continual prayer to God on behalf of man, which was the most important role of cathedrals and abbeys in the mediaeval world so they were taken extremely seriously.

Due to skillful restoration in the late 19th century during which the emphasis was on restoring not improving the building Dunblane Cathedral is one of only four complete mediaeval cathedrals in Scotland. On account of wars and other depredations Scotland has been largely stripped of its mediaeval buildings making Dunblane Cathedral especially rare and valuable. That is why I have placed so much emphasis on the rebuilding of the Cathedral and on Clement who was responsible for its reconstruction. It is not only a local but also a national treasure.

The effigy above beside what was the Altar of the Cathedral in the Middle Ages is almost certainly that of Bishop Clement. Traditionally the builder of a Cathedral was buried in what was considered a place of honour close to the Altar.

(photograph by Len Bovill)

CHAPTER 7

SCOTLAND AND DUNBLANE IN THE LATER MIDDLE AGES AND THE FIRST PART OF THE EARLY MODERN PERIOD 1290 - 1560

The Struggle for Independence from England 1290 - 1353

The Wars of Independence - a brief account

The Wars of Independence between England and Scotland took place because the Canmore dynasty which had ruled Scotland for over 240 years ran out of direct heirs with the death of Princess Margaret, the Maid of Norway, in 1289. This provided an opportunity for Edward 1 of England to adjudicate between rival claimants to the Scottish throne, principally from the Balliol and Bruce families. Balliol was declared the winner and became King of Scotland in 1292. Unfortunately Edward 1 treated him as a puppet which led to war between England and Scotland in 1296 and the complete defeat of the Scots at the battle of Dunbar. Balliol then submitted to Edward 1 and was removed from the throne. For the remainder of his reign until his death in 1307 Edward 1 treated Scotland as a subject province which provoked rebellions led by Wallace and Moray in 1297 and by Bruce in 1306.

After 1307 there followed a period of civil war between the Bruce and Balliol factions and war between Bruce and the English. Many people believe that the Wars of Independence were then concluded with Bruce's victory at the Battle of Bannockburn in 1314. Unfortunately for Scotland this was not the case. While the Battle of Bannockburn was an important victory for the Scots the war continued unabated until peace was agreed between the two countries in 1328. War resumed shortly after the death of Robert the Bruce in 1329. In 1332 Edward Balliol invaded Scotland reigniting the civil war between the Bruce and Balliol factions. Though Balliol was quickly driven out Edward III of England took up his cause and invaded Scotland in the following year and defeated the Scots decisively at the battle of Halidon Hill. As a result the whole of Scotland was forced to submit to Edward III who extended his grip on the country over the next few years. In this period the English King was as dominant as his grandfather had been in the years 1302-06. It was only with Edward III invading France in 1338 that the heat was taken off Scotland with England now fighting on two fronts. Eventually the war subsided in the early 1350s into a series of truces and Scotland's independence was finally established.

Emphasis on the Battle of Bannockburn has also obscured the real nature of the military conflict between England and Scotland. It is fair to say that unless circumstances were extraordinarily favourable as they were at the battles of Bannockburn and Stirling Bridge the Scots could not win an open battle against the English. The English armies were larger, better armed and manned by soldiers who were paid to serve as opposed to the Scots armies which were made up of local levies who were obliged to serve with their superiors as part of their feudal obligations. But the Scots were successful when they avoided open battles and resorted to guerrilla warfare as Bruce did so skilfully from 1309 to 1314. There was of course a reverse side to this equation. The English could dominate Scotland when they invaded with a large army but they could never completely conquer the country. Its geography made it possible for small groups of determined men to continue to resist especially in the heart of Scotland north of the Forth. Even more the English could not afford to maintain a large army permanently in Scotland so once the army went away rebellion and resistance resumed. In short neither side could deal the other a knock-out blow.

A silver penny of King Alexander III (1241-86).

(Stirling Smith Art Gallery and Museum. Licensor www.scran.ac.uk)

The Bishops of Dunblane and the Wars of Independence

At first sight it is difficult to understand why any of the Scottish bishops or clergy would take a strong pro-Scottish position during the Wars of Independence. After all they were officially men of peace and part of an international church. Moreover the main champion of Scottish independence, Robert Bruce, started his campaign for the Crown with the appalling murder of his rival, the Red Comyn, the nephew of John de Balliol, in the sanctuary of the church of the Minorite Friars in Dumfries. Even in a period noted for its brutality the murder of the Red Comyn and especially the place where it was committed were unlikely to make Bruce a favourite with Churchmen.

We have to go back a number of centuries to understand the opposition of the Scottish bishops and clergy to English control of Scotland. Starting in the 11th century the Scottish kings and clerics had been involved in a struggle with the English kings and the Archbishops of York who wanted to annex the Scottish bishoprics into the archdiocese of York. Scotland had no archbishops and was unable to get the Pope to convert one of the Scottish sees into an Archbishopric, the favoured one in Scottish eyes being St Andrews. After much manoeuvring this struggle was resolved in 1192 by Scotland coming under the direct control of the Papacy as its favourite daughter. However were the English to take over Scotland many of the Scottish clergy were concerned that their independence would disappear. Of course there will have been other reasons for their hostility, not least the brutality of any invasion and occupation by a foreign power.

Inevitably given the disturbed state of Scotland during much of period of the Wars of Independence very few records of the activities of the Scottish bishops including those of the Bishops of Dunblane have survived.

Also it is likely that those bishops and clergy who were working for the Scottish cause especially during the reign of Edward 1 did their best to leave no documentary evidence of their actions for fear of reprisal. Even though bishops were not hung drawn and quartered as were members of the nobility who defied the English kings they could face severe retribution. Thus the Bishop of Glasgow was imprisoned for some years following his support of Robert the Bruce in 1306 and because of his persistent defiance of the English kings. Indeed the English could take punitive action against a bishop even without provocation as happened when Edward 1 instructed his son in 1304 to strip the lead off the roof of Dunblane Cathedral because he needed it for his siege of Stirling Castle. As a result any account of the role of the Bishops of Dunblane before and during their episcopacy at this time has to piece together a picture from incomplete sources and by making intelligent surmises.

One of a number of English silver coins found in Cromarty which were minted in 1280 at Canterbury during the reign of King Edward I of England.

(Cromarty Courthouse Museum. Licensor www.scran.ac.uk)

Nicholas de Balmyle, Bishop of Dunblane 1307 - 1319

The career of Nicholas de Balmyle, Bishop of Dunblane from 1307 to 1319, illustrates the problems over sources very well. Geoffrey Barrow describes Nicholas de Balmyle as one of the inner group of men who were trying to frustrate King Edward's plans for Scotland but he deplores our lack of information about his activities. He writes for example about him:

> *"Although this man keeps himself in the background of surviving historical record, we should be doing him no more than belated justice if we recognised that in these years he played a critically important part."*

Nicholas de Balmyle appears first in the struggle over Scottish independence as an auditor on Balliol's side in 1292. Like virtually every other bishop and nobleman he then submitted to Edward 1 in 1296.

This action did not however prevent him a year later from being involved in the crucial election of a pro-Scottish cleric to the vacant bishopric of St Andrews. That year Nicholas de Balmyle was appointed Official at St Andrews, that is he was in overall control of the see after the death of the previous bishop until a new appointment could be made. Here he showed his true colours. Edward 1 was keen to appoint men to the Scottish bishoprics who were pro-English especially at St Andrews which was considered the premier Scottish bishopric. Though he was not a member of the appointing committee Nicholas de Balmyle as Official will have been of crucial importance in ensuring a favourable outcome of the election. Much to the annoyance of the English William Lamberton, the Chancellor of Glasgow, who was strongly pro-Scottish was selected. Together with other pro-Scottish incumbents at Glasgow and Dunkeld and the unofficial leadership of St Andrews this appointment tipped the balance in favour of Scotland amongst the Scottish bishops.

Aerial view of what remains of St Andrews Cathedral – the largest mediaeval cathedral in Scotland.
(RCAHMS. Licensor www.scran.ac.uk)

Next Nicholas de Balmyle was appointed in 1301 to the important position of Chancellor of Scotland in effect in charge of the Scottish legal system. At the time Scotland only had one Guardian, Sir John de Soulis, who was taking the only path open to a Scottish patriot which was to campaign for the restoration of John Balliol as King however remote such a possibility seemed at the time. It will be remembered that Robert the Bruce did not put forward his claim to the throne until 1306. So Nicholas de Balmyle was at the heart of the Scottish government at a time when the chances of Scottish success were possibly at their lowest. Unfortunately because of this we have virtually no records of his tenure as Chancellor. All we know is that he was part of a group of four men suing for peace with England in 1301 and that he visited Rome at least once during his period as Chancellor to argue Scotland's case at the Vatican.

For the next few years there is little record of Nicholas de Balmyle's activities until 1307. Then for a brief period Robert the Bruce was in control of central Scotland. He used the opportunity to ensure that Nicholas de Balmyle, who was already at Poitiers on his way to Rome on diplomatic business, was elected Bishop of Dunblane. It is unlikely that he had to put much pressure on the Dunblane Chapter because Nicholas was already a member of the Chapter and had the support of two strongly pro-Scottish clerics among its membership. They were Master William of Eaglesham who had already been on missions to argue Scotland's case before the Pope and Bruce's friend Abbot Maurice of Inchaffray of whom more below.

Once Bishop of Dunblane Nicholas de Balmyle is likely to have been heavily involved in constructing the case for Scottish independence. A great weakness in the popular view of the Wars of Independence between England and Scotland is that the conflict was conducted solely on the battlefield or by guerrilla tactics thus ignoring the intellectual and propaganda campaign waged by the Scottish clergy at Rome and throughout Christendom to win the argument with the English. It was vital to put forward a convincing case at the Vatican which was the only international court of the time and pre-eminent because of the importance of Christianity in the early 14th century. The Church was much more important at that time than the United Nations today which finds it so difficult to make effective decisions. Of course it was equally important at home to have a convincing case round which Scots could rally. We should not be surprised at this because every major conflict in which one country seeks to control another is decided partly on the battlefield and partly in terms of the arguments employed by each side.

The interior of the Chapter House in Dunblane Cathedral today probably where just over 700 years ago Nicholas de Balmyle was elected Bishop in 1307.

(photograph by Len Bovill)

Barrow's view that this case was prepared by a relatively small group of very able Scots clergy is now generally accepted. It appears that they were in almost continual interaction with the papacy between 1300 and the striking Declaration of Arbroath of 1320 honing a convincing case for Scottish independence in terms that appealed to 14th century men. The case they developed had a number of features which reached their peak in the Declaration of Arbroath as follows.

First, emphasis was placed on what was believed to be the origin of the Scots people namely that they were descendants of Scotia, a daughter of the Pharoah, and after centuries in Greece they arrived in Ireland and finally settled in Scotland. There they drove out the Picts and took over the country. Having a distinguished lineage was essential for establishing a right to independence in the 14th century.

Second, the authors of the case for Scottish independence drew on the tradition that Scotland had a strong connection with St Andrew, Christ's favourite disciple, who it was believed had visited and possibly died in Scotland. In this they were building on their favoured relationship with the Papacy which had been established in 1192.

Third, they drew attention to the brutality of the English in their attempted conquest of Scotland, a theme which will have been familiar to

Modern painting of a Scottish nobleman signing the Declaration of Arbroath 1320.

(National Trust for Scotland. Licensor www.scran.ac.uk)

14th century ears when conquering armies were particularly ill-disciplined and which will have accorded with the experience of many Scots. The behaviour of the English led the Scots to seek a champion who could defend them and they selected Robert the Bruce.

Finally to emphasise that their claim was for freedom for a people not for a royal dynasty they made the first official statement of qualified monarchy in the Middle Ages. They stated that their loyalty to Robert the Bruce and his descendants was conditional on the king and his family not surrendering to the King of England or the English. Were they to do so they would cease to be the lawful kings of Scotland. In the 14th century when kings were thought to be God's chosen instruments this was a very revolutionary theme indeed.

Between 1300 and 1319 these arguments were hammered out in numerous visits to Rome and in many discussions at home, all of which led to statements by the clergy with the King's approval. Nobody knows who wrote the letters to the Pope, the statements by the clergy at home or the Declaration of Arbroath but they are now believed to be the work of the inner group of leading clergy who stood for Scottish independence. As a former Chancellor of Scotland Nicholas be Balmyle would have been right in the centre of this group of clergy.

Maurice Bishop of Dunblane 1322 - 1347

The career of Maurice Bishop of Dunblane 1322-1347 is much easier to describe than that of Nicholas de Balmyle. Maurice was elected Abbot of Inchaffray in 1305 and from the first was clearly a strong supporter of Robert the Bruce. The King was crowned at Scone on Friday March 25 1306 with the support of a significant number of clergy including Maurice. To attend the coronation was a bold step by Maurice. King Robert had two wars to fight and win before he could truly claim the Kingdom. First he had to win a civil war against John Balliol and his son Edward rival claimants to the Scottish crown who had a strong base in the north of Scotland. Second he had to defeat and drive the formidable English out of Scotland. So attending Bruce's coronation as opposed to just staying away was a courageous, possibly a reckless, act by Maurice.

To contemporaries Bruce's fate must have appeared to be sealed by the rout of his army in September 1306 by the English at Methven outside Perth. Bruce escaped with only a few hundred men. It is not known what happened to them immediately after the battle but Geoffrey Barrow is convinced that they received significant help from Maurice and his canons at Inchaffray. He argues that there is no other plausible explanation for Bruce's great generosity to the Abbey later in his reign.

We have already noted how Maurice conspired with King Robert and others in 1307 to elect Nicholas de Balmyle, Bishop of Dunblane. The next piece of evidence places Maurice at the heart of the Scottish Government with Bruce as King. In January 1313 Maurice was given a safe conduct by the English to visit King Edward II to discuss a peace or truce between the two countries. Such a mission is a clear indication of Maurice's closeness to Bruce and leads Geoffrey Barrow to describe him as *"one of King Robert's most trusted and loyal supporters."*

The next year, 1314, saw the famous victory at the Battle of Bannockburn. There are a number of contemporary and near contemporary accounts of the battle. In at least three of them, including the Chronicle of Inchaffray, Maurice is given a central role. He is variously described as hearing Bruce's confession and saying mass with him before the second crucial day of the battle and as being one of a number, or possibly the only priest, saying mass with the whole army. Apparently he also brought a most treasured item to the battlefield from Inchaffray, the sacred vessel in which St Fillan's left arm bone was stored. St Fillan was a much revered Celtic saint. Being cautious Maurice left the priceless bone at Inchaffray. Our 21st realism is somewhat strained by Boecce's much later story that the arm filled with enthusiasm for the Scottish cause found its way without human aid into the casket and then inspired the Scots to victory.

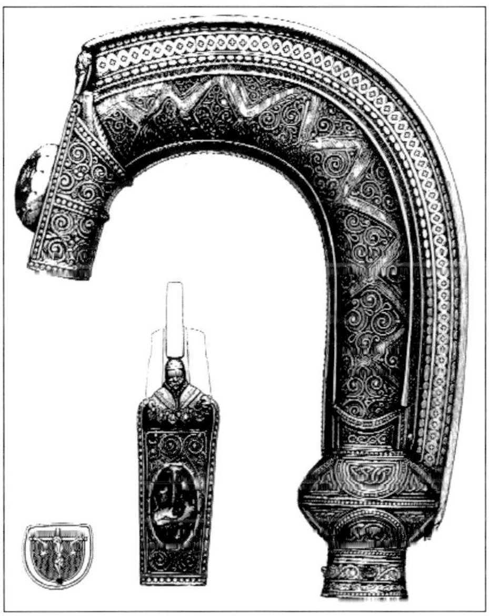

St. Fillan's Casket has not survived but above is part of the 14th century silver case in which St Fillan's crook was kept. The two smaller images are of the other surfaces of the case.

(Gaidheil Alba. Licensor www.scran.ac.uk)

Maurices's support for the King between 1306 and 1314 had a sequel. In 1321 he was a candidate for the Bishopric of Dunblane but he faced stiff competition from Roger de Balnebrich from the diocese of St Andrews and much more seriously from Richard de Pontefract who was proposed by King Edward II. The outlook for Maurice was bleak. In a situation like this the Pope made the final decision and at the time he was favouring the English. Unexpectedly, we don't quite know how, the Pope after a lengthy consideration chose Maurice. The only rational explanation for this unexpected decision is that Bruce intervened decisively for him. So it looks as if Maurice's loyal support for Bruce was in the end appropriately rewarded.

Peace and Consolidation 1353 - 1560

Peace at home 1353 - 1560

Once Scotland had gained its independence it experienced an era of quiet for the next 160 years that was very unusual at that time. There was even very little conflict with England until the cataclysmic defeat at Flodden in 1513 possibly as expensive in young manpower to Scotland in the 16th century as the First World War in the 20th century. Most of the time was spent renewing the truce with England with occasional flare-ups on the border between the two countries. A peace settlement came only in the early 16th century (unfortunately short-lived) when the English crown agreed to drop its claim to overlordship over Scotland - a source of tension between the two countries from the late Saxon period.

At home times were also surprisingly peaceful. Unlike England and a number of other European countries Scotland did not experience a prolonged civil war such as the debilitating Wars of the Roses south of the Border. It is far beyond the scope of this book to attempt a full explanation of the peaceful conditions in Scotland but a number of suggestions have been made by historians which will be considered briefly.

Perhaps most important, it has been suggested that conflict which in other circumstances could have led to civil war was restrained in Scotland by the fear that it might cause English intervention and a renewed threat to Scottish independence. Memories of the savage struggle between the Bruce and Balliol factions which had made it far more difficult to defeat the English and gain independence were still fresh in the minds of the Scots.

Other explanations focus on the relationship between the Scottish King and his people. It has been pointed out that a source of tension in most European countries at this time was national taxation. The prime cause of such taxation outside Scotland was the need to raise armies mainly so that a monarch could capture new territory, the Hundred Years War between England and France being an excellent example. In Scotland such taxation was unnecessary because the Scottish army was purely defensive being made up of feudal levies that is men serving as an obligation to their feudal superiors. They were not paid by the Scottish kings. As a result a major source of tension between the Scottish kings and their people was removed.

Another cause of conflict outside Scotland was the tendency of mediaeval kings to involve themselves in local as opposed to national affairs mainly by the setting up of royal courts throughout their countries. In Scotland, except for cases involving law and order that were a threat to the state, the king stayed out of local administration leaving it to the land-owners and the long established barony courts. So the nobles were left free to run local affairs as suited them best thus reducing possible tension between themselves and the king.

Thus a dynastic dispute like the one between the Stuart kings and the powerful Douglas family did not burst into civil war as occurred in England between the Yorkists and Lancastrians.

An aerial view of Threave Castle built on an island on the river Dee in Kirkcudbrightshire by Archibald the Grim 3rd Earl of Douglas (1369-1390). It was the last Douglas stronghold to fall to King James II in 1455 during his campaign to destroy the power of the Douglases.

(Crown Copyright RCAHMS. Licensor www.scran.ac.uk)

The Contribution of the Bishops of Dunblane to the Government of Scotland 1353-1560

During this period the Bishops of Dunblane made a steady if not outstanding contribution to the government of Scotland both nationally and locally. To start with they acted as a hinge in the important relationship between the Papacy, which controlled the church in Scotland, and the government of the country.

Initially each bishop was elected by the Chapter of Dunblane often after considerable debate and intrigue. The successful candidate then had to go to Rome to be confirmed in the post and consecrated. This process could take some time. Despite their election by the Chapter each candidate had to declare his selection invalid and submit to the Pope's decision. In every case the Pope confirmed the Chapter's choice but only after the payment of a substantial fine. Consecration would then take place and the Pope would send out letters of appointment to the Chapter and clergy of Dunblane.

This process may seem like a charade out of which the Pope gained financially but it was more significant than that. By it every Bishop of Dunblane was brought into close contact with the Papacy and its administration which managed what was a universal church in Western and much of Southern Europe. Familiarity with the 'Curia' ensured that the Bishops were effective agents for the resolution of the church's business in Scotland. They knew how to approach the 'Curia' with requests that were beneficial to the diocese and the country and in return they were trusted by the Pope as agents of the 'Curia'. So each bishop received mandates from the Pope during his period of office. The majority of these related to the settlement of disputes within the diocese but some were of national significance requiring the Bishop of Dunblane to work with other Scottish bishops. For example Bishop William Stephan was asked by the Pope on 1st August 1426 together with the Bishop of Glasgow to consider a petition by King James 1. In it the King requested that the University of St Andrews should be moved to Perth where it was less exposed to attack from the English during wars between the two countries and where the climate was better. So the Bishops through the Popes participated fully in running the church at a national level, an important task given the centrality of the Church in Scottish life.

The Bishops of Dunblane also contributed to the running of secular government at national level. Occasionally they penetrated the very heart of government playing an important part at Court or as time passed in the major organs of government set up by the King. For example at the time when the government was still informal that is revolving round the household of the King Michael Ochiltree, Bishop of Dunblane 1429-1447, was Almoner General to King James 1. He was described by a contemporary source as

"the familiar, the domestic and commensal (eating at the same table) of the king.

This effigy which is in a tomb recess behind the pews beside the south door of the Cathedral is believed to be that of Bishop Michael Ochiltree 1429-1447.

(photograph by Len Bovill)

As such Bishop Ochiltree will have been in a strong position to influence the policies of the king though the informality of the relationship makes it impossible to determine his precise impact.

Once the government of the King became more formal with the development of important bodies like the King's Council, the Privy Council and related officers of state the Bishops of Dunblane were again occasionally prominent. For example Bishop William Chisholm I of Dunblane from 1526 to 1564 was a Lord of the Council and a member of the Privy Council.

At other levels of government, for example Parliament and diplomatic missions abroad the mediaeval bishops of Dunblane were also involved. A study of the records of the Scottish Parliaments reveals that every bishop of Dunblane attended Parliament. Some were closely involved in the actual working of the Parliament. For example Walter de Coventrie, Bishop of Dunblane (1361-71), was a very well qualified lawyer, a Bachelor of Civil Law and a Doctor of Canon Law. It is no surprise then that he served on a number of Parliamentary Committees set up to consider judicial as well as general issues. Bishops of Dunblane were also frequently involved in foreign affairs. A number of them were members of diplomatic missions chiefly to England. Sometimes they would go all the way to the English Court and sometimes they would meet an English delegation at a convenient point. The missions mainly concerned the renewal of the truce between the two countries though there were other issues to be discussed like possible royal marriages and the ransoms of King David II (1324-71) twice and King James I (1394-1437) once. Occasionally they were involved in negotiations with France as the Auld Alliance took increasing shape over this period.

The Bishops of Dunblane and members of the Chapter were also involved in the growing importance of the law during this period. It may be surprising to find a bishop qualified in the law but Canon Law was so important locally, nationally and internationally that it became the norm from about 1400 for bishops to be qualified in it and the Bishops of Dunblane were no exception to this rule. By 1500 the importance of the law began to be expressed in the development of the Scottish legal system. Most significant was James IV's decision to convert the Court of Session from being a peripatetic court to one based in Edinburgh meeting daily. The court's influence grew markedly during the reign of his son, James V. Two clerics from Dunblane were members of the Court of Session at this exciting period in its development. Magister Henry White, a canon of Dunblane Cathedral, became a member of the Court Session in 1516 as did Bishop William Chisholm I in the 1530s. Dunblane clerics also benefited from the increasing number of legal appointments in the King's government at this time with Walter Drummond in the late 15th century becoming the first Clerk of the Rolls (keeper of the king's documents) then a Lord of the Exchequer.

A 16th century oil painting of King James IV (1488-1513).
(National Galleries of Scotland. Licensor www.scran.ac.uk)

The Diocese of Dunblane 1353 - 1560

The general importance of the Bishops of Dunblane in the life of the town and diocese as illustrated by the size of the Bishop's Palace

The importance of the Bishops of Dunblane is demonstrated in physical terms by the size of their palace which was adjacent to the Cathedral. Today little survives except for a sizeable part of the outer wall of the west wing of the palace fronting the river between the Cathedral Halls and the Leighton Library (see below) and some vaults probably for storage which can be seen to the left of the path that runs to the river beside the Cathedral Halls.

The west wall of the Bishop's Palace from the river

The north range of the palace which adjoined the west wing was discovered when the Cathedral Halls were being built in 1903. A vault was revealed 27.43 m by 4.57 m made of red and gray sandstone and running parallel with the wall dividing the church yard from the Cathedral Halls The presence of this vault was confirmed by excavations in August 1994 before the building of the extension to the Cathedral Halls. It is likely that this was the lowest level of the northern range of the palace and was the front of the building.

It is almost certain that there was at least one more substantial range facing west and running parallel to the river since the only visible remains are on this axis. Professor Charles McKean writing in the *Journal of the Society of Friends of the Cathedral* in 1996 has even suggested that this range may have contained in its second storey the gallery of the palace. There is also evidence of at least one tower which would have provided access to the upper floors of the different ranges.

Map showing the likely extent of the Bishop's Palace in Dunblane.

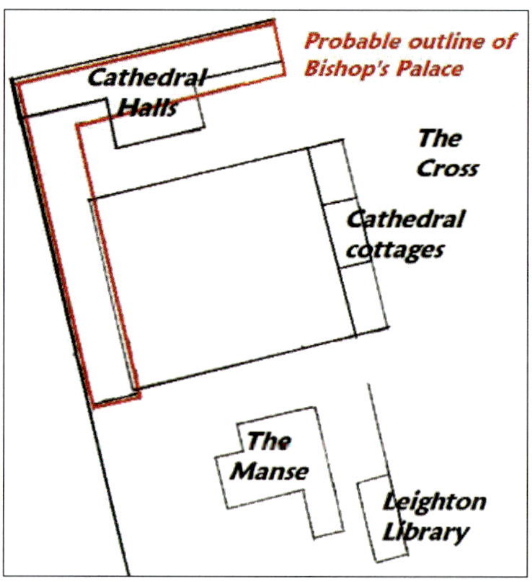

It is clear then that the palace was a substantial building, far bigger than the residence of a normal landowner which would have consisted of a tower for his family and a hall and kitchen separate from the tower. There is no indication when it was built. Below is Slezer's drawing of the west wing of the palace facing the river dating from the 1690s and showing how substantial the building was even after over 150 years of stone robbing.

Slezer's drawing of Dunblane in the 1690s, showing the remains of the Bishop's Palace immediately to the right of the Cathedral.

Providing the daily services at the Cathedral

I remember the shock I got when my history master at school announced at the beginning of a lesson on mediaeval monasteries that their overriding purpose was to pray for mankind, not to heal the sick, not to give alms to the poor, not to provide education, not to create great libraries. They might do some of these things but they were incidental to their main function, praying for mankind. This aim of course applied not only to the abbeys, priories and nunneries of Scotland but also to their 13 cathedrals.

So the main task of the Bishop of Dunblane was to ensure that this obligation of prayer for mankind was honoured. The up to 9 services held throughout each day in the mediaeval Cathedral of Dunblane were to meet this objective. The same routine was undertaken by the monasteries, priories and nunneries but they carried it out in private. In the 13 Scottish cathedrals the services were in public and therefore had to be conducted to the highest possible standards even though they all took place behind the Rood Screen and so were seen only dimly by the local people and visitors in the Nave.

What steps were taken to ensure that the services were conducted to a high standard? This vital duty amongst a lot of others was performed by the Cathedral Chapter although not in person. The members of the Chapter included important office bearers in the diocese as well as church leaders from outside the diocese such as the Abbot of Inchaffray who occupied the post of Precentor of Dunblane Cathedral in perpetuity and the Abbots of

Arbroath and Cambuskenneth who were permanent Canons of the Chapter. All this created problems for the maintenance of services because it would not be possible for these men to be in continual attendance at the Cathedral services. As a result this task was undertaken by junior clergy paid as vicars to substitute for members of the Chapter. Provision was made for them to live in communal lodgings near the Cathedral and for them to receive their meals and upkeep. Unfortunately we don't know where they were housed – indeed aside from the Bishop's palace we can only guess where the other clerics actually lived.

Maintaining the Cathedral – problems

As well as maintaining the services the Cathedral itself had to be kept in a good condition. Given the relative poverty of the see this was not an easy task. The difficulties are illustrated by an Indulgence granted by the Pope to the Church of Dunblane dated 30 October 1419 which arose from a petition sent to him from the diocese. In it the Pope states that the Bishop, Dean and Chapter can no longer maintain the fabric of the Cathedral because of the pestilence (Black Death) which had struck Scotland in 1349, 1362 and 1401 each time killing a third of the population and severely reducing the revenues of the see.

The problems experienced at Dunblane are surprising. Most cathedrals in Western Europe at the time were not only maintaining the internal décor of the building but were in many cases adding to, or altering, their structure. At Dunblane aside from the top two storey's and battlements of the Tower added by Bishop James Chisholm in the early 16th century no significant modifications were attempted and the Bishop and Dean were clearly struggling to maintain the basic building. The difficulties they were experiencing emphasise the poverty of the diocese and the major achievement of rebuilding the Cathedral in the 13th century.

The top two storeys of the Tower added by Bishop James Chisholm 1487-1526 were the only significant additions to the fabric of the Cathedral after its completion in the 1280s.

The explanation of the poverty of the diocese offered by the Pope is also interesting. The Black Death had a major impact on the mediaeval economy. Starting in 1348-49 it swept away approximately one third of the population of Western Europe. Thereafter there were frequent but less severe recurrences of the plague which kept the population at or near to the reduced levels of the mid 14th century for over a hundred years. It is possible that Scotland suffered less badly than other European countries because of its dispersed population and its relatively small urban centres but there is no doubt that the numbers of people living in Scotland dropped sharply. The people who suffered in financial terms from this calamity were perhaps surprisingly the landowners who found themselves short of tenants and labourers. As a result wages rose and tenants were able to negotiate better terms from the landowners. As a major landowner drawing a high percentage of its income from rents the See of Dunblane will have been badly hit by the ravages of the Black Death.

The Black Rat - it has been generally accepted that the Black Death was spread by a flea living on the black rat though this view has been challenged recently.

(Dianne Sutherland. Licensor www.scran.ac.uk)

Finding a way to maintain the Cathedral

The Pope's solution for the crisis is also revealing. First he writes:

> *"To all the faithful on the Feast of St Blane and any of his days and giving a contribution the Pope granted relaxation of penance for 7 years and to the vicar in spiritualities the faculty of absolution to all faithful who confessed to Him and helped the restoration of the church."*

The Pope's statement provides us with clear evidence of the importance of St. Blane for Dunblane Cathedral making it a centre of pilgrimage on his feast day and on other days presumably celebrating major events in the Saint's life. Pilgrimages to places associated with saints were a major feature of the life of the mediaeval church and one of the main ways of raising money. The most famous in Britain was of course the shrine of St Thomas à Becket at Canterbury Cathedral and the best known book about going on a pilgrimage Chaucer's Canterbury Tales. Like other Cathedrals Dunblane will have had a number of relics of the Saint genuine and otherwise.

The rewards offered by the Pope are also interesting. In the Middle Ages it was believed that those who died fell into certain categories. A very small number of people who had led a saintly life went straight to heaven. Of the rest those who had committed mortal sin went to hell for ever and the remainder to purgatory often for long periods. The rigours of this system could be mitigated. It was vital at death to have confessed all your sins to a priest and to have completed the appropriate penance. As a result you had fewer sins to answer for in the next life. Sudden death without confession and atonement led to much more severe penalties in the after-life. As a result people in the Middle Ages were very keen to keep their confessions up to date in case of an unexpected calamity with no priest being near by.

16th century Dutch stained glass depicting The Souls of the Damned in Hell.

(National Museums Scotland. Licensor www.scran.ac.uk)

Perhaps inevitably people began to pay the church fees as part of completing their penance and gaining forgiveness, a system which by the 15th century was organised down to the last detail by the Papacy as we see happening in the Pope's solution for restoring Dunblane Cathedral to its former magnificence. Thus all those making a contribution to the Shrine of St. Blane which would help the finances of the Cathedral were to have free penances for seven years while those giving money towards the maintenance of the Cathedral were to be given absolution from their sins. In both cases the pilgrims and members of the See including the inhabitants of Dunblane were purchasing free penances and absolution from the church.

It is worth mentioning at this point that the growing concern to alleviate purgatory for the dead led to the transformation of the Aisles in the Nave of Dunblane Cathedral during the 15th century. All along the Aisles altars were set up so that priests could say masses for the souls of the dead. These altars which were attached to the walls of the Aisles were wooden. Each of them would have had a reredos behind the cross, that is a wooden panel which might contain a painting or a religious relic. Wooden screens were erected to create small chapels with the altar as the centrepiece. Grooves cut in the base of the pillars in the Aisles enable us to determine the location of these chapels. It is possible that the screens were covered with open carving through which the chapels could be glimpsed. These altars and chapels were set up by important people who endowed them with rents often from land in Dunblane.

Here I am drawing heavily on an article by David McRoberts entitled *Dunblane Cathedral under the Chisholms* which was published in 1971 in the Journal of the Society of Friends of Dunblane Cathedral. I am only going to describe the six altars and chapels in the aisles of Dunblane Cathedral. People who are interested in the nature and locations of the five other altars which lay outside the aisles should refer to David McRoberts' excellent article. The six altars and chapels are indicated in the diagram of the Nave of the Cathedral below.

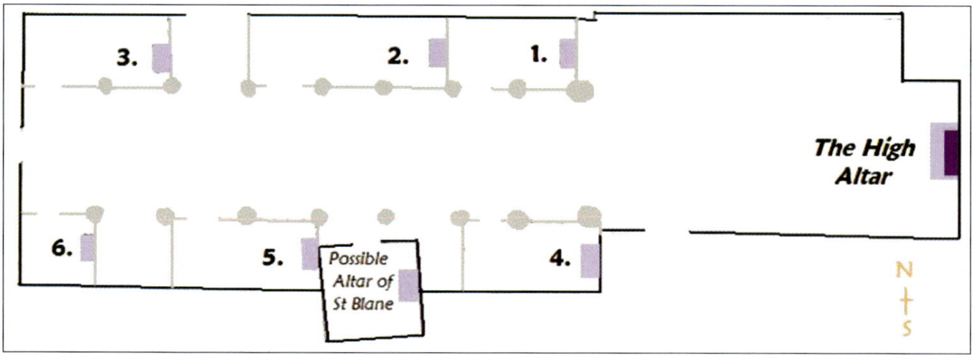

Diagram of Dunblane Cathedral showing the approximate location of six altars.

The first, the Altar of the Blessed Virgin was in the eastern corner of the northern Aisle of the Cathedral. The Altar was set up and endowed by the Stirlings of Keir probably during the 15th century and by the early 16th century had two chaplains. One of them in the middle of the 16th century was Sir William Blackwood who was clerk of the diocesan consistory court and after the Reformation insisted on remaining a Catholic. He is mentioned in the diocesan visit of Dunblane 1586-89 as "a prest in papistrie" who had been excommunicated but clearly to no avail. He was still alive in 1602 aged 82.

The second, the Altar of St Stephen was located in the middle of the northern Aisle. It was probably founded by the Finlaysons of Nether Cambushinnie a farm on the Auchinlay road. Certainly after the Reformation the Finlaysons laid claim to this part of the aisle as their family burial place. It is interesting that Finlaysons lived at Nether Cambushinnie well into the 18th century but by that time they had become tenant farmers whereas when they founded the altar they will probably have been landowners.

The third altar at the western end of the north Aisle was the Altar of St Blaise and the Most Precious Blood. It was probably founded by the Chisholm family who were bishops from 1487 to 1573. Bishop William Chisholm I, appears to have been particularly associated with the Altar adding a dedication to the Most Precious Blood. It is likely at the same time that he installed the two large windows at the western end of the north aisle, presumably to provide more light in the chapel.

Moving to the eastern end of the south aisle there is the fourth Altar, the altar of St Nicholas. It was probably founded by Margaret Countess of Menteith who married as her third husband John Drummond of Concraig.

They were related and were only permitted to marry by the Pope if they agreed to found an Altar in Dunblane Cathedral and if they provided marriage dowries of five silver merks for two poor maidens. St Nicholas was associated with the provision of dowries for poor maidens so it is likely that this Altar is the one endowed by the Countess and her husband. If so this Altar would be a Drummond family foundation.

There was possibly a fifth altar half way down the southern aisle dedicated to St Fillan but there is no surviving record of the patrons of this foundation.

The large windows at the North West corner of the Cathedral which were probably installed by the Chisholm Bishops to provide more light for their Altar to St Blaise and the Precious Blood.

Finally in the western corner of the southern Aisle was the Altar of the Holy Trinity. It is likely to judge by 17th century burial claims that this Altar was originally founded by a family named Farquhar. It may have been the place where the Bishop's Consistorial Court met. In this connection it is interesting that Master Henry White, Official, that is the chief legal officer, of the Diocese of Dunblane endowed a chaplaincy at this Altar in 1533-34.

The Diocesan Church Courts and their business

Aside from maintaining the Cathedral and its services perhaps the most important duty performed by the Cathedral clergy was the administration of the church courts. They were managed by the Chancellor and the Official who were members of the Chapter. Occasionally if a case was very important the Bishop himself would sit in judgement. These courts were respected because their ultimate authority came from the Pope who in the eyes of the people was the head of Christendom. Their significance can be illustrated by an important case in which the church courts in Dunblane can be seen benefitting society as a whole.

In 1380 the Chancellor of Dunblane received authority from the Pope to dispense 20 men and women living in Dunblane from the rules of consanguinity. As a result the Chancellor could permit these people to marry individuals previously barred to them because of too close a blood relationship. For example they were free to marry their first cousins. This ruling may seem at first sight a run of the mill concession necessary in a community that was much less mobile than today and where as a consequence so many people were closely related to each other. It is in the final sentence that the purpose of the ruling is revealed and it is surprising to us. It is as follows:

"so that by arranging marriages between the contesting families an end may be put to the feuds, murders and factions in these parts."

This instruction shows the church using one of the main strategies employed in the Middle Ages to end local feuds whether between families or neighbours which plagued society and was obviously tearing Dunblane apart at the time. Marriages between individuals from the two warring families would bind them together thus ending a feud which otherwise might last for generations.

The church courts also provided general legal services covering civil as well as canon law, that is church law. Unfortunately only one of the pre-Reformation court books has survived from the See of Dunblane – the Act Book of the Commissariat of Dunblane 1552-1555. This book which was studied in detail by Hutchison Cockburn reveals the quality of the church courts in Dunblane. They employed sophisticated legal procedures, they processed cases speedily, up to 20 a day being recorded in this one surviving Court Book and their reputation amongst the laity was obviously high since a lot of people were bringing lay issues to the court. For example the court considered disputes over property and allegations of slander as well as more conventional canon law cases such as matrimonial issues and quarrels over the payment of teinds, the 10% of crops due to the church from everybody in the Middle Ages.

Providing Education

There was one other important service provided by the cathedral clergy, namely a school. Before the foundation of the first Scottish Universities in the 15th century the only education provided in Scotland beyond basic literacy was at the schools attached to the cathedrals and at a small number of schools in burghs like Stirling. They prepared men for the church giving them some proficiency in Latin and as time went on they were attended by an increasing number of laymen wanting to enter the law. Before the Scottish Universities were established a number of these men will have gone to Oxford or Cambridge or continental universities straight from the school in Dunblane. Even afterwards many will have continued their studies abroad after a grounding at a Scottish university. It is surprising therefore that between 1223 and 1586 which is after the Reformation there is no surviving reference to a school or schoolmaster at Dunblane. The reference before 1223 is to a man called Macbele who is described as "Rex Scholarum de Dunblane" i.e. Governor of the Scholars of Dunblane. The reference after the Reformation is to a grammar school in Dunblane. It occurs during a clerical visitation to Dunblane in 1586 as part of a visit to every parish in the diocese. In their report the visitors deplored the decline in the school in recent years and point to a lack of funding as responsible especially for paying the Schoolmaster and for funding poor pupils who were "weilwillit to lerne." There is no suggestion that there had been no school before the Reformation rather a concern that former standards were not being maintained.

Life in the parishes of the diocese

So far we have been considering the very important functions provided by the Cathedral and the clergy associated with it, but we have not thrown any light on what was happening in the parishes of the diocese. The loss of the documents associated with the See make it impossible to construct a precise account of what happened in each parish in this period. However some documents throwing light on the clergy appointed at parish level have survived especially for the 16th century. These sources have been thoroughly examined by J.R.Todd for his Ph.D. thesis on 'The Reformation in the Diocese of Dunblane' and it is on this work that I will be principally drawing.

The top layer of the parish clergy in the diocese were the parsons, usually described as the holders of a benefice which is a church living and includes being in overall charge of providing religious services in the parish. As a result they received most of the income that was due to the parish clergy annually. It is perhaps surprising to us that as the Middle Ages advanced fewer and fewer parsons were involved personally in serving the religious needs of their parishioners. Indeed by the 16th century this was the case in 35 out of the 38 parishes in the diocese of Dunblane. Eleven were held by the Bishop of Dunblane or some official of the Cathedral and 24 by religious houses or their members, nine of the houses being situated outside the diocese. Only three parishes St Madoes, Dupplin and Tulliallan were not in the hands of clergy or religious houses but were controlled by lay landowners. As a consequence it is likely that two of these three parishes in the 1530s and 1540s actually had parsons serving the cure, Mr David Balvaird at St Madoes and Sir John Ker at Dupplin. In the case of the third parish Mr David Panister, the Bishop of Ross, was the parson and was clearly an absentee.

The next layer of parish clergy were the vicars. As their name implies they were originally the deputies or substitutes for the parsons. Despite this by the mid 16th century even the appointment of vicars who did not involve themselves in the religious duties of the parish was becoming the norm. In the case of the diocese of Dunblane the names of only 21 out of 38 vicars can be established for the mid 16th century probably because vicars are less prominent than parsons. The pattern was the same as for the parsons. Eight posts were occupied by officials or ordinary clergy serving the Cathedral, five by officials of abbeys, one by the Bishop and three by pluralists, that is clergy with a number of appointments. For example Mr Robert Herbertson who was Vicar of Aberuthven was also Parson of Ayr, Vicar of Rutherglen and held a chaplaincy. J.R.Todd found it difficult to determine how many parishes were actually served by these vicars and he suggests that it was as few as four though some of the clergy at the Cathedral may have performed occasional duties.

The bottom layer of the parish clergy were the vicar pensioners and the curates who did virtually all the work in the parishes. Vicar pensioners received a small fixed annual salary. One such salary quoted by J.R.Todd for the vicar pensioner of Comrie in the mid 16th century was £10 only. In addition vicar pensioners were allowed to charge their parishioners for the services which they provided. Curates received no salary and had to survive only on fees. Given that the parishes were generally very poor it is unlikely that the vicar pensioner and curates earned much more than between £50 and £75 per annum. Contrast that with the £320 taken from the parish of Abernethy by its parson and vicar together and in return they played no part in providing religious services for their parishioners.

In the later Middle Ages and especially in the 16th century this whole system came under sustained attack. The critics have always appeared to have a strong case. It was certainly grossly unfair that the great majority of the income for the provision of religious services in a parish should go to men who took no part in caring for the spiritual welfare of their parishioners. They simply took the money and with it were free to pursue their careers as church officials, lawyers, academics and in some cases as servants of the king.

By the mid 16th century the critics had further sharpened their case by arguing that the vicar pensioners and curates who actually served the religious needs of their parishioners were so poorly educated that they were incapable of preaching to their flocks and giving them satisfactory religious instruction. There was some truth in this criticism. J.R.Todd has been able to trace the careers of twelve of these vicar pensioners and curates in the diocese of Dunblane before and after the Reformation. The positions held after the Reformation by all except two reveal that they were in fact poorly educated. Ten of the twelve were readers after the Reformation usually in the parish where they had served before the Reformation. Revealingly the post of reader was the lowest in the Reformed Church after 1560 not being permitted to preach or administer the sacraments because of their limited education. Only two of the twelve were promoted above reader, Mr Adam Marshall became an exhorter at Fossaway that is he was permitted to preach but not to administer the sacraments and Sir William Scott at Callander became minister allowing him to perform all the religious functions. Only Sir William Scott survived in post, Mr Adam Marshall being reduced to a reader when examined and failing the test in 1588.

Recently this critique has been questioned. It has been pointed out that the elite clergy played a very important part in mediaeval life. Up till 1450 they were the educated elite of society, and even in the 16th century with a growing number of well educated laymen the clerics were still in the majority. As such they were the leaders of the church intellectually, administratively and legally and of course the church dominated society almost completely. People believed that this life was only a brief and unpleasant interlude before the next life reached by direct entry to heaven or through purgatory if of course an individual avoided dropping into hell for eternity. This whole belief system which controlled every facet of people's lives was developed by the church over centuries. Only in the 16th century was it challenged seriously and then only by a different form of Christianity.

In the lay world, if that is a correct term at a time when religion was so dominant, the influence of the clerics can be seen in the part they played in the King's government as ambassadors, as peace negotiators, in a crisis as advocates for their king's policy at the Holy See, as advisers to the kings on domestic policy, as civil servants especially in the treasury and finally as lawyers. They were probably more valuable to the king than his lay advisers because they did not by their nature have great family interests to pursue from generation to generation and of course with the benefice system the king did not have to pay them while his other advisers and civil servants had to be continually rewarded.

One of eight panels decorating the private apartments of Cardinal Beaton (1494-1546) in his castle at St Andrews. He was one of the last of the senior clerics to play a significant part in the King's government before the Reformation.

(National Museums Scotland. Licensor www.scran.ac.uk)

Even at parish level there has been some reconsideration of the critique. The performance of the vicars in the parish may also not have been as poor as has been subsequently portrayed. They were criticised for not providing their parishioners with sufficient religious instruction in the form of sermons and catechism. But we do not know what their largely illiterate parishioners thought of their performance. It is possible that they looked to the vicars to provide the services associated with birth, marriage and death and above all with absolution from their sins. Also at the annual communion they ensured that the community largely healed its divisions since people who were in conflict with their neighbours, or who had committed major offences against them, could not be admitted to communion without reconciliation and forgiveness. It is interesting that this form of communion was preserved by the Reformed Church well into the 19th century showing its efficacy in healing and reconciling the community. So our traditional view of the failures of the late mediaeval church may be open to question.

The Bishops of Dunblane and the prosperity of Dunblane

The Cathedral, bishops and clergy made a significant contribution to the prosperity of Dunblane. The Cathedral as a centre of pilgrimage and worship, the bishop with his large and impressive palace and the officials of the See and other clergy resident in Dunblane all attracted business to the town and its surrounding area. It is interesting that a report in the late 16th century noted the large number of vacant plots in the town presumably where clergy and people associated with the See had lived before the Reformation. The bishops made deliberate attempts to improve the prosperity of the town. Thus Bishop Finlay Dermoch had a bridge built over the River Allan in the early 15th century, most likely the first bridge at Dunblane unless the Romans built one in the first century AD. The bridge which is just by the Stirling Arms can still be viewed.

Bishop Finlay Dermoch's Bridge at Dunblane today.
(photograph by Len Bovill)

There have been at least two significant additions to this bridge, but if you go down to the bank of the river and look under the bridge you can still see his original construction which was made of yellowish stone. The bridge will have had a great impact on the prosperity of the town since heavy goods could be transported across the River Allan much more easily. The bridge led almost certainly to the construction of the High Street, Dunblane's first bypass! Up till then the main street had been Mill Row along by the river. The new High Street will have attracted new settlers to the town and created greater prosperity.

Probably as a consequence of this increased economic activity Bishop Ochiltree got an Act through Parliament in 1442 erecting Dunblane into a free barony in favour of the Bishops of Dunblane. As a result Dunblane could set up its own market and charge customs dues all of which would be regulated by its own court headed by a Baillie under the ultimate control of the Bishop. Though this new status fell short of the rights of a royal burgh, which included share in the monopoly of foreign trade, Dunblane was now free of interference from any local landowner other than the Bishop. It could develop its position as a centre of trade and economic activity in particular exploiting its geographical position on the border between the Highlands and the Lowlands with the opportunities that presented for trading in Highland cattle. At this stage Dunblane had a weekly market which was held on Thursdays and three annual Fairs on Whitsunday that is 28th May, St Blane's or St Lawrence Day, 10th August and All Hallows Day, November 1st. The town was therefore in a good position to exploit the trade in animals especially through its fairs to which traders would come from all over Scotland. It is likely that the thriving leather industry evident in Dunblane in the 17th century sprang from this time.

Dunblane's Coat of Arms today.

The granting of these privileges raises the difficult issue of Dunblane's status prior to the award of the free barony. In the British Museum there is a seal entitled *"S (igillum) commune Burgi Dunblanensis"* that is *"the common seal of the burgh of Dunblane"*. The seal clearly predates the award of the free barony to the Bishop and in any case calls the town a burgh. There is no explanation or confirmation of this award of burgh status to Dunblane so it appears to be a mystery.

The society and economy of Dunblane 1353-1560
(illuminated by the use of late 16th and early 17th century evidence)

Unfortunately there is little surviving documentation which provides evidence of the state of the society and economy of Dunblane from the mid 14th to the mid 16th centuries. It is possible however to sketch a picture of the period by drawing on later documents mainly from the 17th century for the following reasons. First it can be argued persuasively that the social and economic structure of Dunblane changed very little from the mid 14th to the late 17th centuries. Farming, especially in Scotland, did not alter significantly, if at all, over the period and though there was a small number of inventions in manufacturing they did not seriously affect the process of production. The second reason is the survival of a rich collection of personal inventories for 17th century Dunblane - 260 in all, almost certainly the largest concentration outside the main Scottish cities. It is likely that at one time there were numerous inventories of people living in Dunblane in the 14th and 15th centuries but none have survived. A small number have for the 16th century but they tend to be of people living in the town as opposed to the countryside so only provide a limited picture of life in the parish of Dunblane in the 16th century. However what they do reveal is on the same lines as the 17th century inventories. For these two reasons the lack of change over the period and the survival of the 17th century inventories I have decided to focus on them in this section of the book.

These inventories were drawn up so that the diocesan Commissary Court which was based in Dunblane could confirm people's wills and so ensure the fair distribution of their goods between their heirs. They were confined to moveable goods so in the case of landowners were largely lists of money owed by and to them. More interesting and far more numerous, making up 90% of the total, are the inventories of tenant farmers and artisans. In the case of tenant farmers their holdings in animals and crops were listed and for artisans any tools, raw materials and products not yet sold. Also included were all their debts and any sums of money owed to them. In all cases an estimate of the value of their household possessions was attempted and sometimes for wealthier individuals all their household goods were itemised.

The basic industry in Dunblane as elsewhere in Scotland was agriculture which employed over 90% of the population. As a result an individual's relationship to the land was the crucial determinant of a person's position in the social hierarchy.

Landlords and Tenants in Dunblane 1353 - 1560

Dominant in Dunblane were the landowners. Even the Bishop's undoubted prestige as a church leader was financed and buttressed by his position as a big landowner. In Dunblane the Bishop's estate stretched from the Haining by the Cathedral along the river where the Laighills Play Park is at present, which was probably the Bishop's orchard, and then for over two miles on the western bank of the river Allan through the Auchinlays, Cromlixes and Cambushinnies. The other big estate owners in Dunblane were the Stirlings of Keir. In Dunblane they owned the land from modern Keir House up to Kippenross. Then in the north of the parish they had significant holdings centred on Greenloaning and including the Quoiggs on the east of the Perth Road.

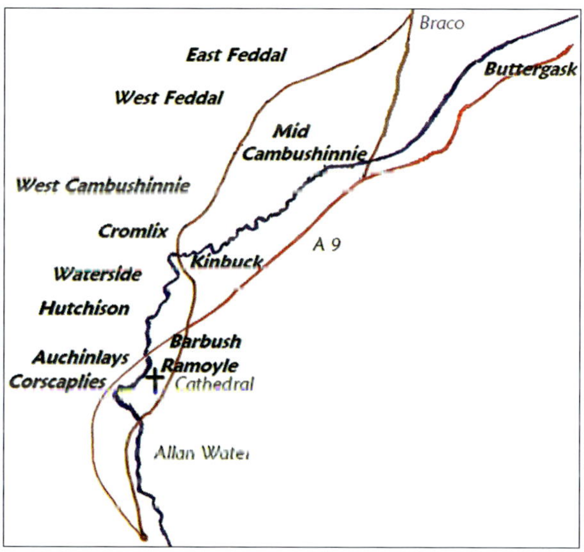

Map showing the main settlements on the Bishop's estate in Dunblane.

Below these two major landowners was a stratum of small landowners each with little more than 300-400 acres, the size of a small farm today, for example the Kinrosses of Kippenross, the Finlaysons of Cambushinnie, the Grahams of Bowton and the Wrights of Drumdruills. This type of small landowner was largely to disappear in the late 17th century bought out by their wealthier neighbours.

Below the landowners were their tenants, most of whom had by modern standards very small plots of land. There appear to have been three strata of tenants. At the top and few in number were men and occasionally women, when their husbands were dead, farming between 100 and 150 acres. Much more numerous were tenants with between 30 and 50 acres. Finally there was a large number of tenants with between five and ten acres, very small holdings even by the standards of the time. This last group inevitably had other means of earning money, either as artisans or as labourers, on the landowner's demesne or home farm.

Almost all of the tenants in Dunblane occupied fermetouns, generally three or four families per fermetoun. The names of these fermetouns are still on the Ordinance Survey map. For example along the Auchinlay road are Upper and Lower Auchinlay, Upper and Lower Cromlix, West, Middle and Nether Cambushinnie and others.

Each of the tenants had a small holding of *"infield"* ground which was near to their houses. Generally this land was heavily manured sometimes being rather graphically called *"muckit"* land on which the most valuable crop, barley, and some of the better qualities of oats, *"white"* or *"croft"* oats, were planted. The remainder of the crops usually poorer quality seed better suited to rough land, variously *"black"*, *"gray"* and *"small"* oats, were planted in the *"outfield"*. The rest of the outfield and the ground after harvest was used for grazing the animals. In addition most of the tenants in Dunblane had access to the moorland above their outfield which was also used for grazing.

It is likely also that in this period tenants in Dunblane made use of the very high land of the Ochils and Trossachs which borders on the parish as shielings. These were pastures in the high uninhabited hills to which a significant section of the farming population of a settlement went in the summer months to give the animals fresh grazing and where they made butter and cheese. It is generally accepted that the majority of those going to the shielings were women and children, the men staying to cultivate

Photograph of the Sheriffmuir hills leading to the sheilings deep in the Ochils.

the crops. Use of shielings was almost universal in Scotland in parishes with access to hills. The only reference to shielings in Dunblane is at a court case in the early 18th century. In it tenants in Dunblane on the Balhaldie and Quoiggs estates bordering on Sheriffmuir are described as finally abandoning their summer visits to shielings in the Ochils during the disturbed period of Civil War from 1640-60. Everybody had to stay on their settlements to prevent them being robbed.

All the tenants owned animals in proportion to the size of their holdings. Cows were kept mainly for milk and cheese and sheep for wool and cheese. It is odd to our taste but in the later middle ages cheese made from sheep's milk was preferred to that from cow's milk. From their inventories it appears that very few tenants kept beef cattle reflecting the low demand for meat. Horses were also kept for ploughing and the carriage of goods since virtually no tenants had carts until the early 18th century. Sometimes when reading inventories it appears that the number of horses kept was very high for the size of the holding; perhaps the keeping of horses was a matter of prestige at this time. Though they were not listed in the inventories because of their low value we know that all the tenants in Dunblane had hens because they formed part of their rental which was almost entirely paid in kind.

Beneath the tenants was a large and shadowy group known as cottars. They were the labourers and servants hired by tenants annually for a small fee of little more than £12/0/0 Scots for a man and £8/0/0 for a woman, a cottage (hence the term cottar) and a small plot of land sublet by the tenant on which to plant crops and keep a cow. Little is known about cottars. Very few of their inventories have survived because they usually had nothing to leave being very poor indeed. Also they were seen by landowners as the responsibility of the tenant so there is little record of them even among estate papers. Only if they fell foul of the church or lay courts is there any mention of them.

To emphasise how poor cottars were it is worth quoting the inventory of a hird (somebody who herded animals) William Drummond who died in Glassingall on 13 December 1610 leaving a wife and daughter. All he had was as follows:

Tua young ky (heifers) pryce of the piece (each) £8/0/0 Inde (Total) £16/0/0
He cofessit (swore - he drew up his own inventory before he died) him to have na utencils (tools) nor domicils (furniture) but only the abridgements (clothes) of his body 20/-

William Drummond is obviously a cottar because he had somewhere to graze his animals and would occupy a cottage with his wife and child. He is desperately poor having no tools or furniture at least none that was worth anything. He did not even have a kist that is a small chest in which to keep his possessions. His clothes were valued at 20/- again depressingly poor when a plaid would be valued at a minimum of £3/0/0. The only reason that there is a record of his goods is that he did have a number of small sums of money owing to him in all £48/0/0. This appears to contradict the impression of poverty but in the early 17th century such debts were often very difficult to collect.

Economic activity in the town of Dunblane 1353 - 1560

The situation was different in the actual town of Dunblane. It is likely that between 1350 and 1560 it was relatively prosperous. It was home to the Bishop and clergy and the Cathedral with its relics of St Blane was a centre of pilgrimage. In addition the town's geographical position meant that its weekly markets and annual fair were well established. The servants of King James IV bought a number of heavy horses in Dunblane to draw the baggage carts on the ill-fated campaign which culminated in the Battle of Flodden. Such a town would have had the usual range of artisans, for example maltmen, brewing ale and whisky, websters, weaving cloth and metalworkers like lorimers and smiths. Also in evidence among the inventories in 16th and 17th century Dunblane, and almost certainly for a considerable time before, were a surprising group of artisans – leather workers of all types.

The leather industry was the second most important industry in the Middle Ages in Scotland, textiles that is wool being the most significant. In the 16th and 17th centuries this industry was well represented in Dunblane. There were skinners and tanners who processed the animal hides as well as sadlers, belt makers and a number of glovers. The skinners and tanners are a particularly significant group because they needed a lot of capital to operate since the hides took upwards of three years to turn into leather that could be worked. First a number of hides would be soaked in a pit of water mixed with lime, bird and dog excrement so that they became soft. Then they were tanned by placing them in another pit of water and covering them with bark. The water leached tannin from the bark which was absorbed into the hide making it flexible and giving it a brown or tawny colour. The process was repeated several times until the hides were ready for use. To judge from their inventories skinners and tanners appear to have lived either in Mill Row or on the High Street and as a result it is likely that the pits in which the hides were soaking would have been on the river bank beside Mill Row where they could keep an eye on them. If so the smell in the centre of the town must have been overpowering. The glovers, sadlers and belt makers will have worked with the leather producing goods for local use and for the growing population of Edinburgh.

Open ground to the north of the Mill Row car park where the pits of the skinners and tanners may have been situated.

How prosperous were the people of Dunblane 1350 - 1560?

Aside from the landowners, elite clergy and leather workers how well off were the people living in the parish of Dunblane at this time? The answer is that they were very poor. It has already been pointed out that the average tenancy was small. Worse the yield from crops and animals compared with today was very meagre. Oats, the main crop in Dunblane yielded three times the seed that was planted and barley, the other crop, sown on the heavily manured infield four times. Today the yield on such crops is at least forty times. The produce from animals was also poor. Over the year in the 14th to 16th centuries a cow yielded about 100 gallons of milk compared with 700 gallons today and the fleece of a sheep weighed only one to two pounds compared with over six pounds today. In addition to these poor yields Dunblane did not have the best land in Scotland. That was in the Lothians, Angus, and parts of Fife, Moray and Caithness which could produce wheat which sold for more than twice the price of oats, the predominant crop in Dunblane. As a result of the poverty of the tenants the artisans who catered for their needs, the websters, mealmakers, brewers, smiths and lorimers were also very poor.

The poverty of the tenants and artisans can be seen from the low value of their personal goods, that is their clothes, furniture and tools as quoted in their inventories. Generally these possessions are not itemised, all that is entered is their overall monetary value, on average £6/0/0 Scots and very rarely above £10/0/0 Scots. Drawing on the occasional pricing of individual items in the testaments this means that tenants and artisans in Dunblane are unlikely to have had more than one suit of clothes and only very basic furniture such as tables and chairs. Their inventories would not have stretched to the possession of beds, not even the cheapest in the 16th and 17th centuries, which were described as fir beds presumably because they were made of fir wood. Certainly none of them would have had box beds which were expensive items. It is likely that their beds were simply sacks filled with straw for a mattress and their clothes for covering. Such beds were still in use among poor people in the Highlands during the early part of the 20th century. Equally poor was their stock of agricultural implements. Very few of the tenants will have had ploughs, carts or harrows, all of which were expensive. It is likely that tenants on a fermetoun jointly owned one plough between them but there is no indication in the inventories that this was the case.

As to housing it is now generally believed that the predominant house outside the towns in Central Scotland was like the Highland black house or a byre house because it included a byre for the animals. Examples of modern black houses can be seen at the Kingussie Highland Museum, at Killin and at Auchendrain close to Inverary though of course the modern version of the black house was more sophisticated than their predecessors in the late Middle Ages. In the 14th to 16th centuries they were simply constructed with a spine of wooden crucks to hold up the roof. The walls would be made mainly of peat on stone foundations and the roof also of peat and heather. The typical black house had effectively two rooms one for the humans and one for the animals that had to be housed during winter. The single room for humans usually had a hearth in the middle of the room for cooking with an opening above to allow the smoke to escape. Conditions were probably better in the town with walls made of stone and proper chimneys in place though the roofs were almost certainly of straw or thatch. Some of the houses will have been of two storeys with four rooms, two up and two down, each occupied by a family. This explains why in old illustrations houses are often seen with stone staircases at the back or front for access to the top storey.

No black houses survive from the 16th century but they may have looked like the 20th century black house in front of Dun Carloway Broch on the isle of Lewes above.
(National Museums Scotland. Licensor www.scran.ac.uk)

Social, personal and legal relationships 1353 - 1560

Social and personal relationships between people living in Dunblane at this time are of some interest. The tendency for families, usually brothers, to occupy one fermetoun and for women, when married, to live with their husband's kin may go back as far as the Iron Age. To judge by the surviving inventories for the 16th and early 17th centuries it is likely that the strong kin structure in the countryside was beginning to dissolve. The same family names appear from generation to generation living in fermetouns but from time to time new names emerge, quite a few of them Highland, which reflects Dunblane's position on the main road south.

Women appear to have continued to live with their husband's kin and according to recent accounts by historians, for example in *The Oxford Companion to Scottish History*, edited by Michael Lynch, to have had virtually no rights when married. They are described as having no legal persona that is not being recognised by the courts as having an existence independent of their husbands. It is also stated that all their property on marriage passed to their husbands. However the last statement appears to be at odds with the situation revealed in the 16th and 17th century Dunblane inventories. For example there is the frequent assertion in inventories that all the goods owned by a married couple were held *"in common."* or jointly owned. It is likely that this state of affairs was associated with the woman having had a dowry at marriage which enabled her husband to purchase stock for their tenancy or materials and tools if he was an artisan. In return the husband and wife held their goods "in common" or jointly giving the wife a strong legal position. An example of joint ownership of goods is that of Catherine Reid who died in May 1583 leaving her husband Finlay Scobie and four children. The family lived in *"Raterne"*, today Rottearns, just beyond Greenloaning on the Perth Road. The inventory is introduced as follows:

"In the first the said defunct with hir said spouse had the time of hir deceis forsaid the goods and gear underwritten of the value and prices following...

Also the laws of inheritance appeared to protect the wife's position on the death of her husband. On his death a widow was entitled to a third of her husband's estate and the children to another third. As a result a husband with a wife and children alive was only permitted to dispose of a third of his estate as he saw fit. It appears that married women's right to property was surprisingly robust.

The role of church courts in regulating property, marital and moral issues and even feuding has already been mentioned. Comprehensive as these courts were their powers did not extend to the regulation of day to day working and trading conditions in town and country. In the countryside these matters were dealt with by baronial courts set up by each landowner to manage their relations with their tenants and even more important between the tenants themselves. The equivalent in the town of Dunblane was the Regality Court which regulated the markets held every week in Dunblane and set exacting trading standards for the artisans and retailers.

We know quite a lot about these courts because they continued in existence until the mid 18th century. In the case of Dunblane there are references in surviving documents to two baronial courts for the land owned by the Stirlings of Keir, one for the tenants immediately around Keir House and one for the tenants of the Quoiggs estate, opposite Greenloaning, in the north of the parish. There is also a court book recording proceedings in the late 17th and early 18th centuries at the baronial court of the estate owned by the Stirlings of Kippendavie. Finally there are surviving records of the proceedings of the Dunblane Regality Court between 1690 and 1710.

In recent years a lot of research has been conducted on the working of baronial courts in Scotland from the 14th to the 18th centuries and it is reasonable to assume that the conditions established for Scotland applied to Dunblane. Historians have been very interested in the management of these courts and in the principles of justice applied in them. Ultimately they were the landowners court; in the case of the Regality Court the Bishop was the landowner. In these courts the landowner could preside over the court in person but in practice he rarely did leaving its management to his Baillie who represented him. In turn the Baillie used the tenants or, in the case of the Regality Court, the artisans to run the court. They provided a procurator fiscal from among their number and burley men appointed by the court to arbitrate in disputes. In the case of the baronial court for the tenants around Keir House one of the ordinary tenants is mentioned as Procurator Fiscal for the court at the end of the 17th century. They were very much people's courts and much of their business was reconciling disputes between the tenants or townsmen.

Their system of justice is unfamiliar to us and there is much that we can learn from it. They had no local prisons in which to place offenders so their justice was based on restitution to the victim and reconciliation between people in dispute with each other. Thus a man who had injured another person, even seriously, had to pay compensation for the injury as opposed to being locked up in prison. So when people quarrelled, an all too frequent event when they lived in close proximity on the same settlement all their lives, they had to be publicly reconciled through the courts. The burley men of the court played a major part in bringing about these reconciliations because their judgement was respected. The whole aim of the court was to preserve good neighbourliness without which these communities would have been unable to survive. Contrary to popular belief these courts were not harsh in their judgements except to outsiders, for example passing highlanders accused of thieving or worse. They could suffer the extreme penalty hence the frequent place-name of Gallowshill in Scottish parishes. According to Barty writing in 1944 there was a *"Gallowshill"* on the Argaty estate in the parish of Kilmadock bordering Dunblane and part of the Auchinlay Road as you leave Dunblane was known as *"Gallow Lane"*.

The Reformation in Scotland and Dunblane 1520 - 1560

The Reformation like the Industrial, French and Russian Revolutions is very difficult to describe. It was brought about by a bewildering variety of causes, not only religious but also political, economic, social and intellectual and it was a European movement not one confined to the British Isles, let alone to Scotland, then on the fringe of Europe. It is even more difficult to locate Dunblane and its diocese within what was an international movement.

It is important then to outline the strategy which will be adopted in this brief analysis of the Reformation in Scotland and Dunblane. The following themes will be described:

1. The state of the Catholic Church in Scotland in the first half of the 16th century
   (a) some signs of health
   (b) significant weaknesses.
2. The campaign of the Protestant Reformers in Scotland and near Dunblane.
3. The last ditch attempts at reform by the Catholic Church in Scotland 1549 - 59.
4. The impact of political events in Europe and Scotland on the Reformation 1517 - 60.
5. The Protestant rising - June 1559.
6. The Reformation Settlement of 1560.

The state of the Catholic Church in Scotland in the first half of the 16th century

Some Signs of Health

Recently historians have pointed to the fairly robust state of the Scottish Church in the first half of the 16th century. They have pointed out that collegiate churches (churches with two or more clergy officiating who are of equal status hence the term collegiate) were still being built and that considerable expense and effort was still being made to enhance the beauty of the interior of churches. Within the diocese of Dunblane two examples are quoted, the superb rood screen at the Collegiate Church of Fowlis Easter and the choir stalls gifted by Bishop James Chisholm 1487-1526 to Dunblane Cathedral. The stalls six of which survive at the west end of the Cathedral are generally agreed to be of a very high standard. The canopies which were designed to protect their occupants from draughts were carved with centaurs and other mythical creatures within rich foliage. All of the seats can tip up thereby providing a ledge on which the cleric attending a service can rest while appearing to stand. As a result they are called misericords or mercy seats.

Other lively developments at the time included Bishop Elphinstone's Aberdeen breviary, the service book of the Church in Scotland. The Sarum or Salisbury use was abandoned for a more Scottish flavour which included the introduction of 70 Scottish saints for the first time. Bishop Elphinstone not only founded Aberdeen University but early in his career was treasurer of the diocese of Dunblane. Equally important was the growth in music at the time with the anthems of Robert Carver which are enjoying something of a renaissance today. Also significant was the steady growth in education at the church schools and at the universities. Especially noteworthy is the Education Act of 1496 which instructed all barons and householders in Scotland to send their eldest sons to learn Latin presumably at Church Schools.

Examples of the superb carving on the Chisholm Stalls at the back of the Cathedral.

(photograph by Len Bovill)

There were also signs of growth and vitality in at least one sector of the 16th century Scottish Church. Though there had been no new monastic foundations since the Carthusian Priory in Perth in 1426 there was much activity among the friars. In all 11 new houses were founded mainly in Scottish towns in the late Middle Ages. The friars were of a high calibre. Unusually for the period they were excellent preachers, including in Gaelic, and they were to provide some of the main champions on both sides of the religious divide during the 16th century. The public all over Scotland continued to give generously to the friars. For example Sir John Stirling of Keir deposited funds with the Observantine friars for the endowment of a daily service at the high altar of Dunblane Cathedral after his death which took place in 1537.

Significant weaknesses

The abuse of church appointments in the Catholic Church in Scotland became wholesale during the 16th century. Right throughout the Scottish Church in the first half of the 16th century senior appointments such as bishops and abbots were almost entirely removed from the control of the chapters and the monks into lay hands.

In the case of bishops and abbots the gift was increasingly in the hands of the King or of important local families. For example King James IV (1473-1513) nominated first his brother James, Duke of Ross, to the Archbishopric of St Andrews to be followed by his illegitimate son, Alexander Stewart, aged only 9, who was eventually killed at the Battle of Flodden. In the minority of James V (1513-42) after his father's death the various rivals to control the country used the appointment of bishops to increase their influence among the Scottish aristocracy. For example the Bishopric of Aberdeen was granted to a brother of the Earl of Huntly, of Dunkeld to the brother of the Duke of Atholl and Brechin to the son of the Earl of Bothwell. These men were not required to be in Holy Orders. Dunblane did not escape being in the hands of the Chisholm family from 1487 to 1573. In the case of the transfer from

An heraldic portrait of King James V (1513-42) and his first wife Queen Magdalene of France. They were married on January 1st 1537 and the Queen died eight weeks later allegedly on account of the bad Scottish weather. It was under James V that some of the worst abuses of clerical appointments took place.

(National Library of Scotland. Licensor www.scran.ac,uk)

James Chisholm to his brother William in 1526 the manoeuvre was accomplished by the legal device of appointing a coadjutor. A coadjutor was literally a helper appointed to the bishop who worked with him for a number of years before the transfer could take place. It is interesting that Ian Cowan, perhaps the chief authority on the Scottish Reformation, reckons that at this time only one appointment that of Robert Reid to the See of Orkney in 1541 can stand up to serious scrutiny. The situation was very similar with the appointment of abbots. Perhaps the most flagrant case was that of King James V who appointed his five illegitimate sons to be abbots of Melrose, Kelso, Coldingham, St Andrews and Holyrood.

At the same time for various reasons the church's role as a landlord changed significantly during the first half of the 16th century. Heavy taxation by the king, uncertainty about the church's future and severe losses because of the war with the English in the 1540s led the church to adopt a different approach to its tenants on church land. Instead of a simple rent land was now feued out to tenants. Initially tenants paid a heavy fine often called a grassum on entry to the feu and occasionally also on the death of a tenant and entry to the tenancy by his heir. At the start therefore the church raised money quickly. But as time went on the advantage shifted to the tenant. The payment was fixed and as the 16th century advanced inflation reduced the real cost of the feu year by year. Also holding a feu gave tenants a permanent right to the land which had not been the case before. Though these processes sound perfectly above board they could be made much more nefarious if the men holding the bishoprics and abbeys feued land to their relatives. Such a strategy could extend to generous leases and occasionally what constituted a gift of land to family and relatives.

The Bishopric of Dunblane suffered badly from such procedures, particularly from the grants made by Bishop James Chisholm and his half brother Bishop William Chisholm I who together were Bishops of Dunblane from 1487 to 1564. The latter has been nicknamed the "Robber" Bishop because of these grants. A major beneficiary was James Chisholm another brother of Bishop William Chisholm I. From 1509 to 1535 a series of grants leased the principal estate of the Bishops, Cromlix, to James Chisholm in perpetuity. The estate included Over, Nether and Middle Cromlix, Over and Nether Auchinlay, Wester Buttergask (near Blackford), Bridgend, Ramoyle and Barbush, all in the parish of Dunblane. Included also was the right in perpetuity to be Baillie of Dunblane which meant that James Chisholm and his successors could collect all the customs dues paid on market days and any fees or fines paid to the Baillie's Court in Dunblane. Another local family to benefit from the grants by the Bishops were the Stirlings of Keir who were in due course to be related to the Chisholms. In 1511 the Stirlings were able to rent the lands of Rottearns and Quoiggs to the north of the parish for a small annual rent. By 1536 they had acquired Glassingall, Mor and Ochlochy on similar terms. In 1542 the tie was to become closer when Jean Chisholm one of the eight daughters of Bishop William Chisholm I (all of them of course illegitimate) became the second wife of Sir James Stirling of Keir. The Bishop undertook to pay the ordinary expenses of the couple for five years after their marriage and arranged for the teinds (tithes) of a number of farms in Dunblane to be paid to them. In return Sir James agreed not to sell or in any way modify the ownership of any of his lands without consulting the Bishop – a limitation that was not to Keir's disadvantage because the Bishop was a very shrewd and successful businessman. Finally just outside the parish of Dunblane in 1560 Bishop William conferred the parish of Ardoch upon Henry Sinclair who married a niece or it may have been a daughter of the Bishop.

The abuse of appointments in the Scottish church and the alienation of church lands had serious consequences for the Scottish Church in the first half of the 16th century. The laity, especially the educated elite, were scandalised by the visible corruption of the church leadership and in many cases their manifest unfitness for the posts they occupied. They contrasted the wealth of the leaders of the clergy with the poverty of the parish priests. Perhaps unfairly they questioned whether the church was serving its parishioners well with, in their view, little attempt being made to instruct the laity in their religion because of the poor quality of the parish clergy. It is likely that the educated laity were very much influenced by the movement coming from the continent of Europe to translate the bible into the vernacular and permit people to find at first hand what God and Jesus had said. If they could not read it was considered vital that they should be instructed by priests using the vernacular bible. The reaction then to the state of the church in the first half of the 16th century was to condemn it on moral grounds. But many of the educated elite also had strong financial reasons for wanting to limit the power of the church if not to replace it by another church. The alienation of church lands by feuing, leasing and gift, such as happened in Dunblane, created a class across Scotland who wanted to secure their ownership of the land they had received from the church and the best way to achieve that aim was to establish a church settlement which would guarantee that ownership. This class of new landowners were especially influential in the Reformation Parliament of 1560 which established the Reformed Church. It is likely then that the crucial opposition of a section of the landed class to the church in the first half of the 16th century was a potent mix of moral and economic issues.

The campaign of the Protestant Reformers in Scotland and near Dunblane

All revolutions need revolutionaries. In the case of the Reformation in Scotland clerics who had been priests, monks or friars in the church were the men who led the attack.

Protestant agitation was slow to emerge in Scotland. Luther's defiance of the Papacy with his Declaration of 1517 against the Papacy is usually considered the point at which serious resistance to the Catholic Church began in Europe. In Scotland there is no evidence even of a sporadic challenge to the church until the late 1530s. The only signs of possible unrest are the reports of the spread of the new literature of Protestantism, particularly Tyndale's New Testament, which of course was in English. Significantly these reports come from Scotland's eastern ports Leith,

Dundee, Montrose, Aberdeen and Kirkcaldy which were in direct contact with North Germany where Luther was active.

The first time the government took serious action against what it viewed as heresy was in 1539 when a number of Acts condemning the beliefs of the Protestants were passed in Parliament. In addition five men were burnt and nine including George Buchanan fled abroad. George Buchanan was born at Killearn and was already tutor to one of James V's illegitimate sons. He was charged with heresy for writing a satirical poem about friars called *Franciscans*. The centre of activity of the five who were executed was surprisingly Stirling, not the major Eastern ports. Two of the five were Black Friars from Stirling who had written a morality play which was performed at Stirling. One, Thomas Forrest, who was a canon regular from Inchmaholm Priory was vicar of Dollar oddly enough in the diocese of Dunkeld, not Dunblane, a reminder of the fragmentation of the early dioceses. He was accused of preaching every Sunday at Dollar from the Old and New Testament in English. The other two who were burnt were a burgh priest from Stirling and the brother of the laird of Arngibbon in Kippen a parish which is in the diocese of Dunblane but only just.

George Buchanan (1506-1582), after Arnold van Brounkhurst. George Buchanan was the first Moderator of the General Assembly of the Church of Scotland, and tutor to three members of the Royal family, James V's illegitimate son the Earl of Moray, Mary Queen of Scots and her son James VI.
(University of St Andrews. Licensor www.scran.ac.uk)

Thereafter throughout the 1540s and well into the 1550s there are no signs of Protestant agitation in the diocese of Dunblane or in Central Scotland. Very much to the contrary, Bishop William Chisholm I is almost certainly the main reason for the diocese of Dunblane remaining staunchly Catholic. He himself whatever his private misdemeanours was a strong supporter of the Old Church and he surrounded himself by men who agreed with him or were very closely related to him.

In his thesis on the diocese of Dunblane during the Reformation J. R. Todd has analysed the careers of the Cathedral clergy after the Reformation and their connections with Bishop Chisholm. Only one member of the Chapter and of the 16 choral chaplains who conducted the services in

Dunblane Cathedral before the Reformation conformed to the Reformed Church after 1560. He was the Dean, Mr Richard Gordon, and he only conformed in 1572, 12 years after the Reformation Parliament. Of course the men on the Cathedral Chapter still received the income from the benefices which they had held before the Reformation after 1560 even if they did not conform to the new Church so they had an income to support them. The other Cathedral clergy, especially the choral chaplains, who conducted the daily round of services in the Cathedral did not have any guaranteed salary after the Reformation yet they did not conform which is very surprising. An additional factor was that some of these men both from the Chapter for example the Chancellor, the Archdeacon and the Official and four of the Canons were relatives of the Bishop as were some of the more lowly choral chaplains. It is likely that the Bishop gave financial support to some of these men especially the choral chaplains.

The Protestants did however make progress in other parts of Scotland especially the Eastern ports. The first town in Scotland where the new beliefs gained a hold was Dundee starting in 1542-43 where the Reformers won over a significant number of the townspeople. Similar trends were evident at Aberdeen with burgesses becoming involved and at Perth. St Andrews was also affected with two factions struggling for control of the town, one Protestant and one Catholic. Significantly the Reformers had little popular impact in Edinburgh. In 1555 when John Knox, already the acknowledged leader of the Reformers, visited the capital he had little popular appeal. He celebrated Communion in private houses and was visited by landowners but was not able to preach in any of the town's churches. Indeed across the whole country even in the mid 1550s the Reformers had only established themselves in a few towns and apparently had no significant influence in the countryside which comprised nearly the whole population in a diocese like Dunblane.

Last ditch attempts at change by the Catholic Church 1549 - 1559

Given the apparent weakness of the Reformers it is perhaps surprising that starting at a Provincial Council in 1549 and continuing in the Councils of 1552 and 1559 significant reforms were introduced by the Catholic Church. Perhaps by 1559 it was already too late since the revolution which produced the Reformed Church was already underway. It is likely that the reaction in the Catholic Church was prompted by the growing disaffection of the laity which had not yet broken out into open revolt. The whole programme was strongly supported by Bishop William Chisholm I of Dunblane who held significant posts in the government during this period.

The changes were broad and quite radical. In 1549 action was taken against the growing custom of clergy living with concubines. At the same time the Church attempted to improve the ability of the clergy to instruct their parishioners. A theologian and canonist were to be appointed by every Cathedral Chapter and every monastery as teachers of doctrine to the clergy and the monks. In addition bishops were required to preach at least four times a year (an indication of how little preaching they had done until then) and parish priests were to preach every Sunday. In 1553 direct action was taken to ensure that instruction took place at parish level to meet the criticisms of the Reformers directly. The Catechism was to be issued in the vernacular and clergy were to explain to their parishioners, the Ten Commandments, the Creed, the Seven Sacraments, the Pater Noster and the Ave Maria. Finally in 1559 the Common Prayer, litanies and evening prayer were to be delivered in the vernacular.

Together these reforms went a long way in meeting the complaints of the critics of the church. Nothing, however, was done to raise the pay and status of the parish clergy, a crucial omission.

The impact of political events in Europe and Scotland on the Reformation

So far with the exception of Luther's defiance of the Papacy in 1517 we have considered only broad trends within Scotland which affected the Church and its critics, the Reformers. It is of course clear that events outside Scotland were essential for the success of the Reformation. They were important from 1517 onwards and especially between 1558 and 1560.

King Henry VIII, King of England 1509-47, after Hans Holbein.

(Lennoxlove House Ltd. Licensor www.scran.ac.uk)

From 1517 there was in North West Europe a slow tide in favour of Protestantism. In North Germany the princes acted to protect Luther from the Papacy with the result that they formed the first Protestant states in Europe. Of equal importance was the English King Henry VIII's break with Rome, together with growing sympathy for Protestantism in the Netherlands, Southern France and eventually Geneva which became the centre of Calvinism, so important for the formation of the Scottish Reformed Church. As a result Scottish clerics sympathetic to reform had many places to which they could go in Europe for refuge and to hone their reforming ideas.

Political trends were especially important between 1558 and 1560 pushing the Reformers to try and seize hold of the country and ultimately contributing to the legitimisation of their new Church by the Reformation Parliament. In England in November 1558 Queen Mary, who had re-introduced Catholicism in England, died and was succeeded by the Protestant, Queen Elizabeth. Immediately this opened the possibility of a Protestant alliance between the English and the Scots if the Protestants were to succeed in Scotland. This threat was appreciated by Mary of Guise, the Regent of Scotland, ruling on behalf of her daughter, Mary, who was being reared at the French court. The Regent wanted to bequeath to her daughter a Catholic Scotland which was closely allied with France. No decisive action was taken by either side for six months. During that time

Elizabeth confirmed her intention to restore Protestantism in England. Meanwhile on the European continent the Treaty of Cateau Cambresis was concluded in April 1559 between France and Spain leaving Henry II of France free to bring active support to Mary of Guise and crush the Protestant party.

The Protestant rising - Summer 1559

The threats faced by the Protestants in Scotland and the hopes of help from England caused Knox to return to Scotland and the Protestant rising to begin in May 1559. Two armies were involved. The Protestants were supported by armed men from Ayrshire and Glasgow as well as local help from sympathetic landowners. Mary of Guise, the Queen Regent, could look to Catholic landowners and some French soldiers for help. During the summer there were a number of stand offs between the two forces. Meanwhile the Protestants gradually took over the main towns sacking the friaries and purging the churches of idolatry helped by the town mobs, or *"rascal multitude"* as Knox called them not without a touch of guilt. Of course from time to time towns changed hands but broadly speaking during May and June 1559 the towns of Dundee, Perth, St Andrews, Stirling and Edinburgh were secured. Throughout this period the number of landowners supporting the Protestant cause was significant with important men like the Earl of Argyll and Lord James Stewart, one of the illegitimate sons of King James V later to become the Regent Moray, coming over to the Protestant side.

It was sometime late in June 1559 that the Reformation reached Dunblane. Barty, basing his account on J P Lawson's *Book of Perth*, gives a lively description of how the Cathedral was stripped of much of its statues and ornamentation by a band of armed men led by the Earl of Argyll and Lord James Stewart. According to this story the intruders interrupted a service being conducted by the Dean of the Cathedral. A lengthy and heated discussion took place between the Earl, Lord James Stewart and the Dean which is reported verbatim before led by Lord James the armed men seized all the relics in the Cathedral and threw them into the River Allan. After this the congregation slunk home leaving the service unfinished.

When this story is traced to its origin in *The Book of Perth* the sources that are quoted are disappointing. It appears that the story was obtained:

> *"from a lady who was a descendant of Principal Tullideph of St Andrews, one of whose ancestors had warmly espoused the cause of the Reformation."*

A further sentence is added as follows:

> *"Where her outline of his story has in any case been filled, it has been by reference to Mr Row's MS, to the local chronicles and to history."*

No detail is provided of Mr Row, his MS, or the local chronicles or which parts of the story were *"filled"*.

The story in the Book of Perth has therefore to be discounted but there is a germ of truth in it. Towards the end of June 1559 the Earl of Argyll and Lord James Stewart with a band of men were moving around stripping churches of their relics, statues and imagery, first in Perth, then in Stirling, though when they got to Stirling the job had already been done by a local mob. In their journey from Perth to Stirling they will have passed through Dunblane and raided the Cathedral. But whether they encountered the Dean and had an exchange with him before the congregation abandoned the service we shall never know nor what passed between them. However it is certain that towards the end of June 1559 the Cathedral was raided and it is likely that all the records of the diocese were destroyed at this time. Thereafter the Cathedral was no longer a Roman Catholic edifice.

John Knox (1513-1572) the leader of the Protestant Reformers in Scotland. Wood engraving after Adrian Vansour 1580.

(Scottish National Portrait Gallery. Licensor www.scran.ac.uk)

The Reformation settlement of 1560

These events were retrospectively legalised by the Reformation Parliament which met in June 1560. The previous month had seen the arrival of English troops in Scotland sent by Queen Elizabeth which secured the withdrawal of French troops thereby removing the last barrier to reform. During the Parliament the break with Rome was confirmed and a Protestant Church was established in Scotland. All services were to be simplified and in the vernacular and ministers were encouraged to use *ex tempore* prayer. Monasteries, friaries and collegiate churches were dissolved and a well paid and well educated parish clergy were to be established. What is now the familiar structure of Kirk Sessions, Presbyteries and General Assemblies was to be introduced though for the time being bishops were left in office though they exercised little power. Apart from a brief challenge by Mary Queen of Scots in 1566-67 the position of the new Protestant Church was not to be seriously challenged during the rest of the 16th century.

Bishop William Chisholm I was staggered by these events. He was too ill to participate in the earth shattering changes of 1559 but early in 1560 it is said that he joined the Regent Mary of Guise when she withdrew to Edinburgh Castle where she soon died. At the Parliament of 1560 he refused to condemn the Confession of Faith of the New Church but was not prepared to approve it publicly. He simply asked for more time to consider the document. Eventually he withdrew to Dunblane and probably in the hope that the tide would turn in favour of the Catholics he appointed his nephew, another William Chisholm as his coadjutor in the Diocese which was effectively nominating his nephew as his successor when he died or gave up the Bishopric. So when Bishop William Chisholm eventually died in 1564 his nephew became the third Chisholm Bishop of Dunblane. He was to fulfil his uncle's wish to see the Bishopric in the hands of a stout Catholic but of course his uncle's main aim to have the Old Church restored in Scotland was never to take place.

CONCLUDING REMARKS

There is no doubt that Dunblane owed much to its superb position astride the only major route linking the north and south of Scotland, the first settlement after crossing the Forth and the last settlement when Scots left what is now recognised as the heart of the old Kingdom of Scotland and entered the Lowlands. Clearly it is Dunblane's geographical position that led to it becoming the centre of a Bishopric through which it played an important part in the history of Scotland up to the Reformation of 1560. Dunblane's role in Scottish history and the need to contextualise Dunblane within Scotland means that this book has been two histories, one of Dunblane and one of Scotland. It is to be hoped that the latter has enlightened the former without unduly confusing the reader.

LIST OF SOURCES

As is normal in books on local history today I have not employed a referencing system in the main text of this book though I have mentioned individual sources from time to time. Instead I am listing below the books and articles as far as possible in chronological order which I have used extensively in different sections of the book. The key to the Journal Abbreviations is at the end of this list of sources

12,500 BC - 410 AD

Books

Armit, Ian, *Celtic Scotland,* (London 1997).
Ashmore, P.J., *Neolithic and Bronze Age Scotland,* (London 1993).
Breeze, David, *Roman Scotland - Frontier Country,* (London 2006).
Fields, Nic., *Rome's Northern Frontier AD 70 - 233,* (Oxford 2005).
Goldsworthy, Adrian, *The Complete Roman Army,* (London 2003).
Harding, D.W., *The Iron Age in Northern Britain,* (Abingdon 2004).
Main, Lorna, *First Generations – The Stirling Area from Mesolithic to Roman Times,* (Stirling 2001).
R.C.A.H.M.S., *Survey of archaeological finds and surviving buildings in Dunblane.*
Wickham - Jones, *C.R., Scotland's First Settlers,* (London 1994).
Woolliscroft, D.J., and Hoffmann, B., *Rome's First Frontier – The Flavian Occupation of Northern Scotland,* (Stroud 2006).

Articles

Barclay, Gordon J., Brophy, Kenneth and MacGregor, Gavin, Claish Farm A Major Neolithic Building at Callander, *History Scotland, vol. 2 no.1 (2002), pp.22-25.*
Breeze, David J., Why did the Romans fail to conquer Scotland? *PSAS, vol. 118 (1988), pp.3-23.*
Christison, D.J. and Cunningham, J.H. Account of the Excavation of the Roman Station at Ardoch, Perthshire undertaken by the Society of Antiquaries in 1896-97, Scotland, *PSAS, Third Series, vol. viii (1897-98), pp.399-421.*
Cockburn, James Hutchison, The Celtic Cross in Dunblane, *JSFDC, vol vii (1956), pp.77-82.*
Gordon, A., A cist at Dunblane Cathedral, Perthshire, *JSFDC, vol. xii (1976), pp.34-36.*
Holden, Timothy G., and Sheridan, Alison, Three cists and a possible Roman road at Barbush Quarry, Dunblane, Perthshire, *PSAS, vol. 131 (2001), pp.87-101.*
Mackie, Evan W., Impact on the Scottish Iron Age of the discoveries at Leckie Broch, *GAJ, vol.14, (1987), pp.1-18.*
Morris, D.B., Mammalian remains found in a peat moss at Dunblane, *TSNHAS, vol.xv (1892-93), pp.104-107.*
Robertson, A.S., The Roman Camps on Hillside Farm, Dunblane, *GAJ, vol.i (1969), pp.35-36.*
Woolliscroft, D.J., More thoughts on why the Romans failed to conquer Scotland, *SAJ, vol. 22.2 (2000), pp.111-122.*
Woolliscroft, D.J., and Hoffmann, B., The Roman Gask System Tower at Greenloaning, *PSAS, vol. 127 (1997), pp.563-5.*

The Dark Ages 410 - 1000 AD

Books

Anderson, A. O., *Early Sources of Scottish History AD 500 - 1286,* (Edinburgh 1922).
Anderson, A. O. and Anderson M. O., eds., *Adomnan's Life of Columba,* (Oxford 1991).
Barty, Alexander B., *History of Dunblane,* (Stirling 1944).
Bede, *Ecclesiastical History of the English People,* (London 1990).
Broun, Dauvit, Finlay, R.J., and Lynch, Michael, *Image and Identity The Making and Re-Making of Scotland through the Ages,* (Edinburgh 1998).
Broun, Dauvit, *Scottish Independence and the Idea of Britain from the Picts to Alexander III,* (Edinburgh 2007).

Foster, Sally M., *Picts, Gaels and Scots: Early Historic Scotland,* (London 2004).
Fraser, James E., *From Caledonia to Pictland Scotland to 795,* (Edinburgh 2009).
Cockburn, James Hutchison, *The Celtic Church in Dunblane,* (Dunblane 1995).
Lynch, Michael, *The Oxford Companion to Scottish History,* (Oxford 2001).
R.C.A.H.M.S., *Survey of archaeological finds and surviving buildings in Dunblane.*
Smyth, Alfred P., *Warlords, and Holy Men: Scotland AD 800-1000,* (London 1984).
Woolf, Alex., *From Pictland to Alba 78 -1070,* (Edinburgh 2007).

Articles
Wilkinson Brian, Scotland's Rural Past, *History Scotland, vol. 10 no. 2 (2010), pp.11-13.*

Early Mediaeval Scotland 1000 - 1286

Books
Barrow, G.W.S., *Kingdom of the Scots, Government, Church and Society from the 11th to the 14th century, (Edinburgh 2003).*
Barrow, G.W.S., *Kingship and Unity Scotland 1000 - 1306,* (Edinburgh 1981).
Barty, Alexander B., *History of Dunblane,* (Stirling 1944).
Cockburn, James Hutchison, *The Mediaeval Bishops of Dunblane and their Church,* (London 1959).
Lynch, Michael, *The Oxford Companion to Scottish History,* (Oxford 2001).
Neville, Cynthia J., *Native Lordship in Mediaeval Scotland The Earldoms of Strathearn and Lennox,* (Dublin 2005).
Oram, Richard, *David I the King who made Scotland,* (Stroud 2004).
R.C.A.H.M.S., *Survey of archaeological finds and surviving buildings in Dunblane.*

Articles
Cockburn, James Hutchison, Fasta Dunblanenses, *JSFDC, vol. i (1931), pp.25-33, (1932) pp.27-40,(1933) pp.23-35.*

Late Mediaeval and Early Modern Scotland 1286 - 1560

Books
Barrow, G.W.S., *Robert Bruce and the Community of the Realm of Scotland, (Edinburgh 2005).*
Barty, Alexander B., *History of Dunblane,* (Stirling 1944).
Cockburn, James Hutchison, *The Mediaeval Bishops of Dunblane and their Church,* (London 1959).
Commissariot Testaments for Dunblane, 1539 - 1650.
Cowan, Ian B., *The Mediaeval Church in Scotland,* (Edinburgh 1995).
Cowan, Ian B., *The Scottish Reformation Church and Society in 16th century Scotland,* (London 1982).
Grant, Alexander, *Independence and Nationhood 1306 - 1469,* (Edinburgh 1984).
Knox, John, *History of the Reformation of Religion in Scotland,* (Edinburgh 1949).
Lawson, J.P., *Book of Perth,* (Perth 1924).
Lynch Michael, *The Oxford Companion to Scottish History,* (Oxford 2001).
McKerracher, A.C., *Portrait of Dunblane 1875 - 1975,* (Stirling 1992).
McKerracher, A.C., *The Street and Place Names of Dunblane and District,* (Dunblane nd).
R.C.A.H.M.S., *Survey of archaeological finds and surviving buildings in Dunblane.*
Todd, J.R., *The Reformation in the Diocese of Dunblane,* (unpublished Ph.D. thesis, University of Edinburgh,1973).
Wormald, Jenny, *Court, Kirk and Community 1470 - 1625,* (Edinburgh 1981).

Articles
Cockburn, James Hutchison, John Row, a local boy who became Papal Nuncio and a Scots Reformer, *JSFDC, vol. ix (1965), pp. 145-147.*
Cockburn, James Hutchison, Fasta Dunblanses, *JSFDC, vol. i (1931), pp.25-33, (1932), pp.27-40, (1933) pp. 23-35.*
Hall, Derek W., The Bishop's Palace, Dunblane, Excavation and Survey, *SAJ, vol. 22-23 (2000), pp. 69-81.*
McRoberts, David, Dunblane Cathedral under the Chisholms, *JSFDC vol. xi (1971), pp.37-52.*

Todd, John R., Pre Reformation Cure of Souls in Dunblane Diocese, *Innes Review, vol. 26 (1975), pp.27-42.*

McKean, Charles, The Chanonry of Dublane, a reconnaissance, *JSFDC vol. xvii (1996), pp.78-84.*

Cathedrals and Church Architecture 1000 - 1560

Books

Binding, Gunter, *High Gothic,* (Taschen 1992).

Clifton Taylor, Alec, *The Cathedrals of England,* (London 1967).

Duby, Georges, *The Age of Cathedral Art and Society 980 - 1420,* (London 1981).

Fawcett, Richard, *Scottish Cathedrals,* (London 1997).

Stoddard, Witney S., *Art and Architecture in Mediaeval Times,* (London 1972).

Toman, Rolf, Ed., *The Art of Gothic Architecture Sculpture and Painting,* (Konemann 1998).

Articles

Connor, Neil, St. Rule's Church St Andrews and early stone built churches in Scotland, *PSAS, vol.124 (1994), pp.366-379.*

Dunlop Mrs., (Cameron Annie), Life in a mediaeval Cathedral, *JSFDC, vol. iv (1945), pp.70-86.*

Fawcett, Richard, The 13th century rebuilding of Dunblane Cathedral, *JSFDC vol. xviii (1999), pp.51-55.*

Journal Abbreviations

GAJ Glasgow Archaeological Journal.
JSFDC Journal of the Society of Friends of Dunblane Cathedral.
PSAS Proceedings of the Society of Antiquaries Scotland.
SJA Scottish Journal of Archaeology.
TSNHAS Transactions of the Stirling Natural History and Archaeological Society.

INDEX